Praise for *A Perfect Season*

"Great stuff! **A Perfect Season** *is a must read for parents, coaches, umpires, and league officials. Dan challenges all of us to make sure our priorities align with the kids' desires to play for fun, to learn, and be with friends. He clearly shows that when we work together we can create a great youth sports experience for our kids, teams, and parents!"*
– **John Malkin**, Competitive Baseball League Official

"**A Perfect Season** *is an enlightening read about winning in the game of life. Dan goes deep on the importance of shaping and developing our youth, preparing them for the competition ahead on the diamond and beyond. He illustrates the powerful impact our behaviors have on others and reminds coaches and parents what's most important about youth sports and how to give our kids the best possible experience."*
– **Greg Nielsen**, former college athlete, parent of youth athletes, CEO Great Plains Regional Medical Center, and 1980's Little League legend (in his own mind)

"**A Perfect Season** *is a 'must' read for all youth coaches. Although the 'Fun, Learn, Compete' concepts are simple, Dan shows why they aren't easy in today's win-at-all-costs world of youth sports. It is a guide and reminder that sports really are about the kids — something all coaches and parents need to keep top of mind."*
– **John Henderson,** Youth Baseball and Football Coach

"Dan Clemens's passion for baseball is obvious, but more than that, he is dedicated to teaching — to touching the future through the metaphor where he is called "coach" by a group of 12-year-old boys. I've personally coached a great deal of competitive youth sports, and Dan's messages about preparation, communication, priority-setting, focus, and understanding in **A Perfect Season** *are packed with wisdom, compassion, and power. This book will be a cherished gift for any adult involved in youth sports — coaches, parents, league officials, umpires — anyone. Buy a box of them, and share them widely. The world of youth sports, and our youth, will benefit significantly."*
– **Robert S. Tipton**, author, *JUMP! - Get Unstuck, Extraordinary Life Breakthroughs Through Innovative Change*

"As a tournament director, I see the critical need for coaches to have the right priorities for our youth teams, and Dan is right on track with the need to carefully monitor the health of young arms. **A Perfect Season** *is a page-turner – I didn't want to put it down!"*
– **Larry Tenenholz**, Tournament Director, Gold Glove Youth Baseball

A Perfect Season

A Perfect Season

A Coach's Journey to Learning, Competing, and Having Fun in Youth Baseball

Dan Clemens

QUIET PATH

A Perfect Season — A Coach's Journey to Learning, Competing, and Having Fun in Youth Baseball
by Dan Clemens

Publisher: Quiet Path Books

Books may be purchased by contacting the publisher at:
info@quietpath.com

Original Pencil Illustrations: Janet Clemens

Cover and Interior Design: NZ Graphics, Inc.

Editor: John Maling (Editing By John)

Clemens, Dan, 1967 —
A Perfect Season

Library of Congress Control Number: 2010911425

ISBN: 978-0-9828707-2-3

10 9 8 7 6 5 4 3 2 1

Printed in Canada

 Printed on 100% post-consumer waste paper

1) Sports 2) Baseball 3) Coaching

To
my loving and supportive home team,
Bev, Rachel, and Alan

For
the next generation of baseball coaches

Table of Contents

Part III — April

Part IV — May

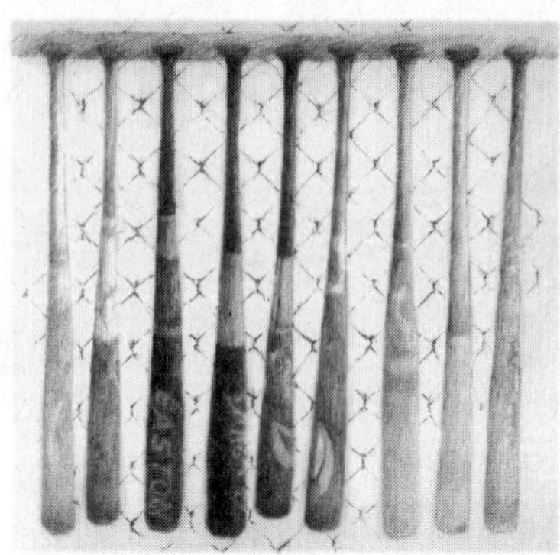

Foreword

For the last 38 years I've had the privilege to teach the game of baseball to thousands of kids as a varsity high school coach. The energy and passion these players bring to the field is contagious . . . it's really tough for me to have a bad day at work!

One thing that differentiates my program from many others is that we don't focus on winning — believe it or not, accruing victories is not a major goal. Certainly we want to win, but winning, we believe, is a byproduct of development. As a result, we emphasize three things: play hard, execute the fundamentals we've learned, and have fun.

This focus may sound a bit strange given the success of our program over the last four decades. After all, we've won seven state titles in Colorado, including five in a row in the late 1990s and finished runner up five other years. And, a couple of years ago I celebrated my 600th career high school victory. Even though it's fair to describe Cherry Creek as a winning program, our mindset is on development. When we do that, winning takes care of itself.

Consider one year my team won 51 straight games. It started in the spring high school season and we cruised through most of the summer season undefeated. In those few months our players learned to compete, gelled as a team, executed fundamentals, and developed keen baseball instincts and the confidence to excel at a high level. It was great fun!

Without a full team of well-developed players, though, a streak like that wouldn't have been possible. What was it that drove 51 straight victories? Obviously a lot of hard work — the kids earned it. But at a deeper level, before the long hours my coaching staff and I spent with them in the batting cages and on the diamond over several seasons, it's important to think about how they arrived in my program.

For this successful group of kids, the building blocks were in place. They had youth coaches who toiled for many years to put them in position to enjoy future success. As a result I received freshman players that were fundamentally sound and knew how to compete. Most importantly, though, baseball passion oozed from their pores because the game was fun.

In short, they'd been fortunate to have seasons like the one Dan Clemens describes in *A Perfect Season.* Dan's book is an excellent behind-the-scenes tour of coaching youth baseball. He does a wonderful job of reminding coaches and parents to focus on three key things that drive baseball and personal development: learn, be competitive, and have fun. As we look into the heart and mind of a youth coach, Dan shows us how to avoid the pitfalls, helps us rejoice in the triumphs, and guides us through the unpleasant. *A Perfect Season* is a voice of reality.

Although Dan writes about his experience with 12-year-olds, much of what he says is of value to all levels and ages of ballplayers. His story will immediately resonate with youth coaches, and those of us at the high school level will gain insights to help us better relate to the youth teams that feed our programs. He challenges all of us to revisit our priorities.

Unfortunately, after working with coaches and players from all over the country, my experience is that far too many high school kids — and their parents — are obsessed with the college scholarship or the pro contract that might follow. They are so focused on a destination that, let's face it, likely isn't going to be reached, they miss the joy in the journey itself.

Here are the cold, hard facts. More than 90 percent of the kids who play in high school will go no further. Their youth and high school experience will be it … how do we want them to remember this time? Of the kids that are fortunate to play at Division I in college, only 5 percent will get drafted to play professionally. That's right, many D-I college programs do not have a player drafted in a given year. And, of those very few young men that do sign a professional contract, less than 10 percent will ever step on a major league diamond during a game.

Don't get me wrong. Playing college or pro ball is a great dream that many of us have shared. It can be an effective motivational tool. But it shouldn't be consuming. This is what I'm teaching at the high school level in one of the more successful programs in the country — 300 of my kids have gone on to play in college and 75 others have been drafted professionally, 15 in the first round.

Despite that success, the most important question is: how has baseball helped them prepare to be better parents, spouses, friends, and employees? Ultimately the development we're after as baseball coaches extends beyond the diamond. We hope that the kids can apply the lessons they learn on the field directly to life. Part of my challenge at the high school level is to help kids and parents learn to have a healthy relationship with the game. Baseball is part of life, not the other way around. Hopefully, they'll see that executing fundamentals, playing hard, and having fun is a good methodology off the baseball field too.

Here's another cold, hard fact. As a high school coach, it doesn't matter to me what a kid has accomplished in the youth game. Wins, batting averages, championships, and the status of playing in so-and-so's world-class youth program are, to me, meaningless material accumulations. Hopefully these things brought enjoyment to the kid, but I'm much more interested in what kind of player and person has developed in those precious years between ages five and 13.

I'm often amazed when parents talk and behave with certainty that their 10-year-old will get a college scholarship. They seem to structure their lives around, and pin their sense of enjoyment on this hope. However, the research is clear . . . playing 80 games in a win-at-all-costs environment isn't healthy for anyone — especially the fifth grader. Here's a tough-love message for parents and coaches: the pressures to win, skewed priorities, and bad behavior means we lose great kids and exceptional coaches. Unfortunately I see good people, young and not-so-young, leaving the game far too often.

What we need is youth coaches instilling in kids a deep passion for the game, demonstrating how to win and lose, developing their baseball fundamentals, and showing them how to work hard and learn. These are the raw materials . . . it is then my job to take their God-given ability and, as they mature into adults, mold them into the best player and person they can be. That's how the relationship between youth and high school programs should work.

That's why I tell youth coaches to teach the fundamentals rather than make a heavy investment in winning. I encourage parents to focus on the journey, not the destination. I say to kids, you should wring every bit of enjoyment you can from playing as long as you can. Treat every practice, game, pitch, ground ball, at-bat, or even inning on the bench as a learning opportunity to make yourself a better player — and person. Do that and the game will take you further than you can imagine.

Dan shows us how to do this in *A Perfect Season.* You'll immediately feel his passion for baseball and you'll both laugh and grimace at the lessons he learns throughout his journey. You'll walk away with nuggets to make your coaching and parenting efforts more successful. But most importantly, Dan will make you think. He'll challenge you to consider how your actions and words impact kids and suggest that you do some healthy introspection of your own motives and priorities.

As you read *A Perfect Season* I think you'll better appreciate the tremendous opportunity and responsibility we have coaching the great game of baseball.

Marc R. Johnson

Marc Johnson
Cherry Creek High School Varsity Coach
Baseball America National High School Coach of the Decade for the 1990s
Head Coach of U.S. National 18-and-under team for 2004 Olympic Games

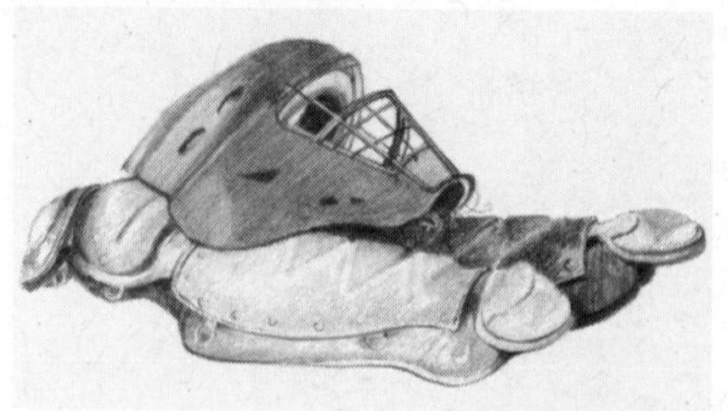

Introduction

Achieving Perfection

Alan and I arrived at the park about an hour and a half before the game, our last of the season. I parked in a space overlooking the field and sat in the car for a moment as Alan gathered his jacket, hat, and sports drink in the back seat. He was about to play in the 12-year-old World Series league championship, and tonight's event was the culmination of a great season. It would provide his team the opportunity for perfection. As head coach I knew we had earned this title shot, having practiced fundamentals, drilled instruction, and emphasized having fun for the last five months. The kids responded by playing hard, winning games, and maintaining a great attitude on and off the field. They had enjoyed the experience.

Indeed, we had earned this opportunity. In the 35 games since March, we posted a 14 wins and 4 losses record in the league while winning one and placing second in another of five weekend tournaments. But this game had more meaning than the others. It stood as an obstacle, a last chance to apply what we had learned and a final test of what we could be.

Stepping out of the car, I did a few quick stretches to get the blood flowing in my aging arms and legs after the 25-minute drive to the park.

Doing my best to keep my legs straight, I optimistically grabbed for my toes but barely reached my ankles. Admittedly, I had lost a step or two in the 20 years since high school.

I took a deep breath and paused for a moment to enjoy the late-afternoon blue sky and the sun beginning to set in the west. Earlier in the afternoon it had rained lightly — a brief shower that tempered some of the heat and washed the dust out of the air, leaving the unmistakable summertime smell of ozone and vivid colors on the field. The grass was green, the dirt a uniform burnt umber, and the stark white of the foul lines framed the field perfectly. Surveying the orange, red, and purple clouds of the sunset I mumbled out loud in homage to the old beer commercial, "It doesn't get any better than this."

I not only felt the excitement, pride, and anticipation for my son and team to play in the World Series, but also a deeper happiness and satisfaction of being alive. It was gratitude as a father and coach to be in this position. Ultimately I felt a sense of appreciation to be living in a country and playing a game that both provide freedom and opportunity for great achievement while rewarding hustle and hard work. Another deep breath, a thought of thanks, and then I began unloading the gear from the trunk of the car.

Our team warmed up for the game as usual, 11 players and one coach throwing in the outfield grass in pairs perpendicular to the left field foul line. While each kid rotated through a few cuts of batting practice with wiffle balls, I pulled aside Nick, our starting pitcher, and explained the need to relax and do the things he had done all season that had made him and the team successful.

"Throw strikes, challenge hitters, and have some fun," I told him while I unwrapped a new white baseball from its plastic bag and placed it in his outstretched hand. "Have fun and savor this opportunity. Go play the game like you can and give us a chance to win."

I stayed with him as he warmed up in the bullpen, not only to offer encouragement and feedback on his pitching mechanics, but also to calm my nerves a bit. The stands were filling with family, friends, and players and coaches from the other eight teams in our league.

I was nervous. I wanted great things for the kids and hoped that each would perform at his best. As coach, I wanted to make the right decisions to let our kids have a chance to win. Despite the fact that I'd played the game into college and had been coaching for six seasons, I still felt a pesky fear under my veneer of confidence . . . I could screw this up.

I watched our infielders take a last round of ground balls. Brandon went to his right, backhanded the three-hopper, twirled and made a perfect throw to the chest of the catcher. The smack of the ball hitting the glove and small puff of dust erupting from the mitt confirmed that we were focused, prepared, and ready. It was game time.

Huddled at the far end of our dugout, the loudspeaker interrupted my last few pre-game instructions, "May I have your attention please. The North Metro League is proud to present the 12-year-old World Series Championship between the Grizzlies and the Yellow Jackets."

I turned towards the press box behind home plate and saw the announcer holding a microphone and reading from a sheet of paper. He introduced the players, pausing briefly so each kid could trot out of the dugout after he heard his name and line up along the baseline while the spectators cheered. Some kids tipped their caps while others simply gave their teammates high-fives and fist-bumps as they went down the line and took their spot. After an instrumental version of the national anthem on undersized speakers, the umpire stood at home plate, and, in a slightly hunched pose vaguely reminiscent of a Norman Rockwell painting, yelled, "Let's play ball."

We were the home team and, after a quick "Yellow Jackets" chant, our kids sprinted out to their positions showing an excitement equal to the magnitude of this game. Nick held them to one hit and no runs in the top of the first — a great way to start. In the bottom half of the first inning we scored a run on a single by our leadoff hitter, a stolen base and then a double. They tied it in the second inning on a walk, a stolen base, a ground out and a sacrifice fly to deep center field.

Neither team scored in the third, but in the fourth inning we broke out for three runs on four hits and an error by their shortstop. They got one run back in the top of the fifth, making it 4 - 2. In the bottom half we loaded the bases but didn't score — a missed opportunity that I hoped wouldn't cost us later on. The game moved to the top of the sixth, the last inning, with the good guys clinging to a two run lead.

Their leadoff hitter hit the first pitch of the sixth inning off the fence in right center field and circled the bases, sliding into home just ahead of the throw. His inside-the-park homerun quickly filled the ballpark with tension . . . nobody out and the score now 4 - 3. The momentum was all theirs. Players from both teams were fully engaged and parents were standing with hands clutched and jaws clinched. Their next batter got a hit and I made the short walk out to the mound and took the ball from Nick. Having thrown 75 pitches he was running out of gas. I pointed to Bobby and he made a quick trot from right field to the mound. I handed the ball to this side-arming lefty who had been our ace reliever much of the season. As he took his eight warm up pitches I told him to relax and do what he'd done all year — throw strikes, keep the ball low and let the defense do the work. He'd heard me say it before, "Make them earn anything they get."

Bobby got the first batter to hit a routine ground ball to Brandon at shortstop. He fielded it cleanly and flipped it towards second base . . . a tailor-made double play. However, it doesn't always turn out like you draw it up in your mind . . . Brandon's throw was wild and it sailed into right field. Both runners advanced, putting them at second and third with nobody out and the score 4 - 3. The opponent's dugout and fans erupted in cheers and encouragement while our side of the field was in silent shock.

I quickly called timeout and trotted back out to the mound to help Bobby and the defense regroup. All four infielders, pitcher, and catcher huddled at the mound looking up at me through worried eyes. They were visibly shaken and quiet, waiting for me to say something meaningful to get them back on track. They needed a boost to their confidence, not a reprimand.

Often in situations like this it's not so much what you say, but that you say something and say it well. They needed to hear confidence in my voice and feel that I believed a positive outcome was not just possible, but probable. Although I was feeling frustration and wondering how things could fall apart so quickly, I had to calm nerves, instruct on strategy, and then motivate to make the next play. Knowing exactly how to rise to that "Gipper" type level of motivational speech is much easier when you're not rehearsing it on the way out to the mound. The perfect words come to you very quickly the next day or the next inning, but in the heat of the moment, the mind can often go completely blank.

"Guys, everyone take a deep breath and relax, we're still ahead in this game and it is the sixth inning," I started, not having anything else in mind to say. I paused for a moment to better read the faces of the players. Brandon's head was down, having just made the throwing error.

"Brandon, forget the last play, man," I continued. "You've nailed those types of plays all year. You're one of the best shortstops in the league and I hope the next guy hits the next ball to you because I know you're going to make the play."

Brandon picked up his head. He was still disappointed, but he was moving out of the past and into the present, which was a really good sign. If he came around, so would everyone else.

"Look, we've been the best team in the league the last 10 games. We've beat this team twice this year. All we have to do is do the things that have gotten us to the World Series here tonight. Make good pitches, make good catches, and make good throws. They still have to beat us. We aren't going to give it to them. Everyone dig deep here, expect the ball is coming to you and know what you are going to do with it."

Now I had to tell them what to do with it. "I want the infield in even with the bases so if a ground ball is hit to you, we're throwing it home to keep the runner on third from scoring the tying run. Also watch for the bunt — they may try to squeeze. Everyone clear on that?" I asked. Five nods and a "Yes, coach" from Brandon affirmed we were on the right track. I now turned to the pitcher.

"Bobby, take a deep breath, relax, and trust your defense — every one of these guys wants a chance to make a play and get us out of the inning. If the batter squares to bunt, throw it high and tight so it's a tough pitch to lay down, okay? Throw strikes and let's get out of here."

My stomach in knots, I turned and walked back to the dugout. With a quick glance to the stands I saw the same stress and tension I was feeling in the bodies and faces of 15 other parents.

Bobby threw a terrific changeup to their next hitter and he popped it up on the infield. Alan made the catch at third for out number one. Bobby struck out the next batter on a fastball low and away. Two outs. This brought their cleanup hitter to the plate. On the first pitch he hit a hard, sinking line drive into left centerfield. Anthony got a great jump on it, running to his left and dove for the ball.

Baseball truly is a game of inches. It's a cliché, but it's true.

The ball hit the grass about six inches short of his outstretched glove and then bounced over and beyond . . . a hit that scored both runners. Andrew was backing up Anthony in centerfield, grabbed the rolling ball, and fired a strike into second base where Zach tagged out the batter trying to stretch it into a double. But the damage was done — they now had the lead 5 - 4 going into the bottom half of the last inning.

Our kids jogged off the field, heads down and discouraged. We gathered the team near the entrance to our dugout for perhaps our final huddle of the season. Coach Sam told them not to hang their heads and not to quit. Full of energy and confidence he reminded them of how many times they had come from behind throughout the season.

I told each one to relax and do his job. "Nobody needs to hit a homerun," I explained. "We need to be patient hitters. Make the pitcher throw you strikes and hit the ball hard somewhere — just like you have all season. Be aggressive but smart on the base paths and look to the coaches for signs on every pitch. We're playing for one run here, so we may be stealing and bunting to get in position for someone to step up with a big hit. Be ready for anything guys … this is what it's all about! This is fun! We're going to win this!"

Sam ended the pep talk, saying, "Come on guys, they've given us their best and all we have to do is score two runs. We can do that no problem!"

Brandon, who had made the throwing error, put his hand in the middle of the huddle and yelled to his teammates, "Yellow Jackets on three" and counted us down to a loud cheer to break the huddle with confidence. The kids were rowdy and excited as our first few hitters pulled on their helmets, adjusted batting gloves, and swung their bats in front of the dugout.

I walked slowly towards the third base coaching box, trying to take a few deep breaths and calm my nerves a bit. The tension in my stomach restricted the air from reaching the lower third of my lungs. "Get a runner on and give your hitters a chance to win this thing," I thought to myself as I heard the last few bars of John Fogerty's "Centerfield" crackle thinly over the loudspeaker.

Bobby led off by drawing a walk on eight pitches, fouling off three good strikes. Jason was up next. He had struggled most of the season, hitting about 150 points below everyone else on the team. We'd tried many different things to make him a more successful hitter, but this level of baseball was testing the limits of his ability and his confidence was low. Throughout the season he quickly would get down on himself for making the slightest mistake, and failure was often a foregone conclusion even before he stepped into the batters box.

As Jason started to walk towards the plate from the on-deck circle I called timeout and jogged down the baseline to talk to him. I put my hand on his shoulder and turned him away from the field so the defense wouldn't hear what I was about to say.

"You are exactly who I want up right now, Jason," I said smiling. He looked at me somewhat puzzled and skeptical.

I'm sure he was thinking, "Yeah, right you want me up there. I'm the worst hitter on the team and the game is on the line. Why would you want me up there?"

Without hesitation I explained, "We need someone who can lay down a really good bunt and get Bobby to second base in scoring position. You are the guy. You've got a good eye at the plate and you are a good bunter. You're going to do this. Now wait for a strike, lay one down, and run as hard as you can to first." I patted him on the back and walked back to the third base coaching box.

This day Jason rose to the challenge of his situation, but again not exactly how you draw it up in your mind. I ran through the signals, indicating bunt so Bobby at first would know the play. The first pitch was a fastball high and inside and Jason pulled his bat back and jumped backwards. The umpire yelled, "Strike one!" as he firmly jutted his right arm out to his side.

Jason was upset believing it to be out of the strike zone. Our fans moaned and awarded the umpire a reasonable amount of grief before turning attention back to Jason with some much needed encouragement. I ran through the signs, again calling for a bunt.

Jason watched the next pitch hit the dirt for ball one. Again I ran through the signs. This time he squared and put down a perfect bunt, a slow roller up the first baseline. The ball started to curl slightly. In a sick twist of fate it seemed to bounce on a small pebble and kick to the right . . . it went outside the chalk and the catcher pounced on it.

"Foul ball!" yelled the home plate umpire who was in perfect position, standing on home plate with mask off. The umpire at second base motioned to Bobby that he'd have to go back to first base. Jason was frustrated. He stood a little more than half way to first base with his hands on his hips, head down and shoulders slumped. Instead of seeing this as an almost-perfect bunt, he saw it as failure. I jogged down to home plate, picked up his bat off the ground and handed it to him as he trudged back to the batter's box.

“Jason, just get a hit.” I said. “Get tough and get a hit. Just think about hitting the ball hard — go do what you can do. Hit the ball like you did against the Grizzlies two weeks ago when you had your best game of the season.” I didn’t wait for him to reply. I turned and ran back to my position.

After the umpire called the pitcher’s next offering a ball bringing the count to two balls and two strikes, I gave the steal signal to Bobby. The pitcher went into his stretch and then threw to the plate. Bobby had a great instinct for reading a pitcher’s motion and as soon as the right-hander’s left heel came off the ground, Bobby immediately took off. The second baseman’s job was to take the throw from the catcher, so he left his position and started running towards second base too, leaving a hole on the right side of the infield. Jason swung late at the pitch and hit a routine bouncing ball right to where the second baseman would have been. The ball trickled into right field and Bobby kept running, making it to third base without a throw. A perfect hit and run! Cheers erupted from our side of the stands and every kid was standing and yelling in our dugout. Jason stood triumphantly on first base, relieved and smiling. We now had runners at the corners with the tying run 70 feet away and nobody out.

Anthony was up next and the first pitch was in the dirt and squirted away from the catcher. It was too close to home plate for Bobby to score from third, but Jason was able to advance to second base. Now the winning run was on second base with nobody out. Momentum was all ours! The game, however, can change very quickly. Anthony popped up to the shortstop for the first out and Andrew struck out for out number two.

This brought Alan to the plate with two outs, the tying run at third, and winning run at second base. Alan was having a great season, leading the team in hitting, playing solid defense, and pitching well. He was exactly the kid we wanted up in this situation — he'd delivered all year with the game on the line. But it is a scary thing as a parent and coach to have your kid in this spot. You feel enormous stress as the coach of what the situation means to the team . . . then multiply it by three or four for what you feel as a parent. Alan stepped into the batter's box with the chance to tie or win the game and appeared to be much calmer and relaxed than I was.

He was over-anxious and swung at a pitch over his head for strike one. The next pitch was a ball and the third offering was a fastball inside. Alan turned on it, and with a picture-perfect swing, crushed the ball. The third baseman watched helplessly as the ball rocketed over his head. Again the baseball gods reminded us of how thin a margin there can be between success and failure. The ball soared well past the depth of the left fielder but hit the grass about one foot outside the foul line. Rats!

The pitcher got a new ball from the umpire, rubbed it down and appeared to be sighing relief. He likely wouldn't throw a fastball inside to Alan again. He thought he had Alan right where he wanted him, but my son had become a smarter hitter this season and was pretty sure the pitcher would throw the next pitch on the outside part of the plate.

The 12-year-old's next and last pitch of the season was a fastball away and Alan was waiting for it. He slapped it sharply over the second baseman into right centerfield. Bobby had already started jogging in from third base with arms raised and scored the tying run. Although Jason was one of the slower runners on the team, he had a determined look on his face and was chugging hard towards me at third. I didn't hesitate in waving him in to score because I knew it would take a perfect throw from the right fielder to get him.

The right fielder ran in on the ball, picked it cleanly out of the grass and came up with a good throw, a one-hopper to the catcher slightly up the third base line. Jason started his slide outside the line and rolled over on his stomach swiping the plate with his right hand as the catcher dove, barely missing Jason's arm with his tag. The umpire yelled, "Safe!" Before the dust even started to settle we streamed out of the dugout, unsure of whom to hug and tackle first, Jason for scoring the winning run, or Alan for the clutch hit that drove him in. We ended up along the first baseline, a pile of 11 ecstatic kids and three relieved coaches celebrating a 6 - 5 World Series championship.

Perfection.

It doesn't get any better than that. A dramatic come-from-behind World Series win with an unlikely hero getting a critical hit and then having my son drive in the winning run.

Perfection.

Well, at least that's how I envisioned it when I put the team together the previous September.

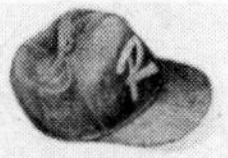

Part I

The Boys of Summer

Not Exactly a Slice of Paradise

Perfection. Ahhh, yes.

I mean, a coach can dream of perfection, can't he?

The reality of our last game, however, was unmistakably different.

Our final game was not played for the World Series championship. Rather it was a matchup of two teams eliminated from the playoffs trying to end the season on a high note. The weather was iffy, spitting rain throughout, and a persistent wind made it unpleasant to be outside without a jacket. The field itself was in bad shape. Several puddles of irrigation water stood in the lowlands of the outfield grass, evidence that poorly-adjusted sprinklers had experienced a long season of neglect. The infield had not been dragged and you could begin to replay yesterday's game by looking at the cleat marks and holes dug by players the day before. The chalk lines had faded and second base was caked in mud.

Our starting pitcher showed up late and one kid forgot his hat. Another got hit in the side of the head with an errant throw while warming up and it was about that time that I realized I had lost a name piece for the magnetic lineup board that I hung in the dugout. Yep . . . a pretty typical pregame routine for the good old Yellow Jackets.

We lost 9 - 2 . . . our first five batters of the game reached base safely, scoring two runs with the bases loaded, only to see the next 18 batters get retired in order. In the fourth inning we did get a hit with one out. I called for a hit and run . . . and we executed almost to perfection. Andrew broke from first and Brandon hit the ball hard. It was a wicked line drive right at the first baseman . . . who caught it and stepped on first for an easy double play.

In the field we committed several errors, and on one particularly embarrassing play reminiscent of tee-ball, helped the other team clear the bases by making three overthrows ... the cutoff man, second base and home (after the batter touched home plate I started to walk out to visit the mound and, in a calm but exasperated tone said to the umpire, “If the ball ever stops rolling, may I have time, please?” His nervous laugh indicated that he both had a sense of humor and felt my pain).

After the game things actually got worse. We had our usual team/family huddle at a picnic table behind the field. As I finished my talk and shook a few hands of thankful players and parents, my disgruntled assistant coach’s wife started screaming at me. As the other players and families ran for cover, the duo condemned me for a month of perceived ills to which I had subjected their son and family. I listened patiently for almost 10 minutes, but when the attacks became personal, I said something I now regret and walked away to end the conversation. His wife, however, continued the barrage, chasing me back to my car where, mercifully, a posse of other parents rescued me with the offer of dinner and a beer. I got in the car and let out a big sigh . . . the monumental effort of coaching for the last six months was over. The end was here and it didn’t look, sound, or feel like I had imagined.

So why the title, *A Perfect Season*? Obviously we didn’t win every game. In fact, we were far from it. We finished 9 - 9 in the league, sixth place out of 10 teams, and 14 - 29 overall including tournaments. Despite the record and one angry set of parents it was perfect. Not in the strict definition of "without flaws," rather, it was perfect because it was exactly what we needed.

Every kid came to the team needing a positive baseball experience. My son and one other had a difficult season the previous year as outsiders joining an established core team with too much yelling and little opportunity to play the positions they wanted. Two other kids had their skills and passion for the game atrophy on a team that went 1 - 17 and received no helpful instruction all year. Valuable practice time was, incredibly, spent on teaching a few of the kids how to run . . . not run the bases . . . just run. Another player quit his team towards the end of the prior season because he was tired of being yelled at all the time. Five kids were moving up from the instructional league to this competitive level and needed the opportunity to learn new skills and adjust to the faster pace of the game.

Before the season began, our collective of 11 players and their families decided that we wanted three things from the experience:

1. to have **fun**,
2. to **learn**, and
3. to be **competitive**.

We reasoned that if you're having fun it is much easier to learn, and you'll find a way to be competitive. **Fun, Learn, Compete** would be how we measured success throughout the season and the three goals would guide our decisions on and off the field.

And it worked.

Amazingly well. With the exception of the assistant coach's son, every kid had fun. In fact, several of them said they'd never had so much fun playing baseball. One had preferred golf and skiing to baseball but by the end of March he and his parents had rekindled their passion for the game. Another hadn't really liked the game much up until this year — it was a filler season for his other sports, but he became more and more "jazzed" about baseball as the season wore on. Several parents said their kids were now hooked on the game for life.

All of this was evident by watching the kids. Body language and enthusiasm reveal when they are having fun and when they aren't. Throughout 43 games our kids smiled, laughed, hustled, worked hard, made new friends, won, lost, committed errors, and made fantastic plays . . . and through it all they had fun. In fact, I would argue that we had nearly as much fun as if we had experienced the dreamy 14 - 4 season and World Series championship I described at the beginning.

The kids also learned the game. Every kid progressed in most, if not all, areas of the game. No matter the starting point, at the end of the season each player was several rungs higher on the performance ladder. Pitchers learned good throwing mechanics, how and when to throw a changeup, and to cover first base on a ball hit to the right side of the infield. Fielders, who in March were having trouble judging fly balls, were making running catches in June. Players who were unsure of where to throw the ball learned how to think ahead.

Don't get me wrong. This wasn't a Hollywood script where a bunch of losers and malcontents found their groove, and, against all odds, won the league. We still booted grounders (a lot of them), dropped balls, and made horrendous overthrows. Our record bears that out. But every player learned about the game, themselves, and how to deal with disappointment, loss, and failure. They also learned to win and gained confidence in both themselves and their teammates.

It showed.

And usually we were competitive. Although we lost 29 games and a few were lopsided affairs, we had a chance to win many of them (or at least we thought we did). We eventually learned not to throw in the towel when we'd get behind early and how to put teams away when we had the chance. We won seven of our last 10 games. Many kids would have given up on a season where the playoffs were out of reach halfway through. Instead, our kids continued to play with passion and we learned to compete.

When you measure success against what each of us needed, and by the three goals we wanted to accomplish — **fun, learn, compete** — our season was pretty darn close to perfect.

Paradise Lost

Seasons like I've begun to describe and idyllic experiences like the one that opened the book don't happen by chance, and in fact, they don't happen very often. Our societal norms are built around winning. From the world of business to academics, television poker tournaments, finding a parking space at the grocery store, spelling bees, and even backyard BBQ horseshoe games, we focus on winners and winning. We consciously and unconsciously equate winning with happiness, however just like the Beatles counseled, happiness and love can't be bought or won. Much more attention is paid to the stories of winners with the hope of unlocking the secrets to their success. But as we'll see in later chapters, winning comes with a price. It's a sacrifice that parents and coaches are willing to pay, but, unfortunately, most kids don't see or want the dividends.

The high value we seem to place on winning, impacts the quality and variety of role models coaches have to help them determine what to value and how to act. Professional and college sports are about big business and high school isn't far behind. The coaches that win get attention, prestige, and long-term contracts. They are featured in magazines, interviewed on TV, and honored at banquets. Losers, or even those that don't win enough, are soon looking for work. While youth sports is supposed to be about something different, the system of rewarding wins above all else is pervasive and influential. You don't have to look beneath the surface to see the flaws in this system.

In the United States between 40 and 60 million kids play organized sports each year. And of the 2 to 6 million coaches leading these teams, 85 percent are dads coaching their own kids and less than 20 percent have received any type of training on how to be a coach. Society, other coaches, and parents chant, "win, win, win," and baseball coaches dutifully load up on drills, push the kids hard for several days a week, and do whatever it takes to win. Most, however, neglect a critical part of their coaching duties: aligning their goals and priorities with what is wanted and needed by the kids they will lead. This is something they must do before their journeys begin.

This is a toxic combination and a recipe for disaster . . . untrained and misguided parents leading teams of impressionable kids pressured by parents, their peers, and a win-at-all-costs culture . . . people snap. The Positive Coaching Alliance recently published its "Bottom 10 Moments in Sports" which included sheriff's deputies restraining a coach of a sixth grade girls basketball game who got ejected, threw a clipboard, and almost incited a riot; a football coach of an 11-year-old team is caught on video shoving the face mask of a player on the other team while shaking hands after the game; a former major league pitcher being removed from the stands of his daughter's fifth grade basketball game for yelling profanity at the officials; and a parent pointing a gun at the husband of a girls soccer coach during a dispute over playing time at a game for seven- and eight-year-olds. Clearly, coaches and parents drive, perpetuate and feel a pressure to win.

This results in a disturbing trend. By the age 15, nearly 80 percent of kids have quit their sport, according to a report by the Center For Kids FIRST in Sports, which cites research from Michigan State's Youth Sports Institute, the Minnesota Amateur Sports Commission, and the UCLA Sports Psychology Lab. The reasons? The report indicates the top seven reasons kids quit organized youth sports are: losing interest, not having fun, too much time, coach played favorites, coach was a poor teacher, got tired of playing, and there was too much emphasis on winning. It also said that 45 percent of kids surveyed said that had been called names, yelled at, or were insulted by coaches.

The report also revealed the top reasons kids play sports . . . to have fun, improve their skills, stay in shape, do something they are good at, enjoy the excitement and challenge of competition and play as part of a team. Winning was last on the list.

It's About the Kids, Stupid

This points to a huge rift between kids who play the sport to have fun, learn, and be with friends and the priorities of coaches and parents bent on winning and the time, commitment, and pressure that accompanies it. It's only the coaches and parents who get the immediate gratification from winning. The kids

Two Major Problems Youth Coaches Face

1. Gap in priorities between what parents and coaches want and what kids want
2. Deficiencies in how coaches deal with two types of day-to-day issues:
   a. Strategic decisions
   b. Events of the moment

don't place the same value on it and, as a result, pay the price. This discord means kids, parents, and coaches are often trying to achieve different things and speaking different languages. This is problem number one.

Problem number two is the deficiency in how many of us deal with the day-to-day events and strategic decisions that every coach (and parent) will face. Consider how success (defined how you like — winning, having fun, learning, growing, being competitive, etc.) hangs in the balance.

Strategic Decisions

Coaches are faced with many decisions about lineups, recruiting, determining the league to play in, which tournaments to enter, how to structure a practice, who to have pitch in certain games, when to bunt or steal, when to pull a pitcher, and how to handle difficult parent issues (just to name a few). Each of these has the potential to make for a successful experience . . . it also has the potential to cause conflict, frustration, and anger.

Events of the Moment

There are also any number of things that will happen before, during and after the games that will force the coach to act. A player will make an error, an umpire will make a bad call, a hitter will strikeout for the fifth time in a row, a parent will make an offhand comment, a kid will swing at a 3 - 0 pitch, the first baseman will drop an easy throw, a pitcher will give up a homerun, the batter will miss a bunt signal, a runner will forget to slide, you'll lose the game, or, my personal favorite, the outfielder will not throw to the cutoff man.

In each of these situations a coach must do something. Even doing nothing is doing something and sends a message. The cumulative effect of his individual decisions and actions will determine how much success and enjoyment the team experiences throughout the season.

The question is, coach, are you going to act in a way that simply eases the pain or frustration of that moment, or are you going to act in a way that furthers your larger priorities and goals? **Will you *React* to the event, or will you *Respond* to the possibilities of the whole situation?**

Respond* vs. *React — there's an important distinction but we tend to use the terms interchangeably. So what's the difference between a Reaction and a Response?

React

A *Reaction* is a reflex — an impulsive action based on an awareness of, and a solution for, only a narrow slice of the situation.

Reactions are often an attempt to dodge pain or grasp for pleasure. It's all about what is happening in front of ***me*** right at the moment. I see, I *React.* I hear, I *React.*

Something happens and it catches our attention . . . we feel compelled to act on this because it is new, strokes my ego, frightens me, is urgent, feels good, is dangerous, is appealing, or otherwise appears important in that moment. But the more we remain locked in on this item, the tougher it is to remember our long term goals or the outcomes we desire for that situation. We have a choice of what we focus on, and even more critical, what we decide is important enough to act upon. When we act based solely on this burning thing in front of us, we're in *React* mode. Our fixation on the urgent, painful, or pleasurable, short-circuits a "big picture" view

> ***REACT***
>
> **A *Reaction* is a reflex — an impulsive action based on an awareness of, and a solution for, only a narrow slice of the situation.**

and we act on this narrow slice of the situation rather than weighing its value or importance against our longer-term goals and objectives.

It's actually pretty easy to lose sight of the achievements we desire. Thousands of distractions and details seduce us away from focusing on what's most important. We're engaged in the game, focused on the situation, the strategy, the next play, and the next inning. Everything happening at that instant seems to be yelling, "I'm important! I'm important! Deal with me now! Deal with me now!" In addition, parents, kids, coaches, and umpires have their own priorities, and want a slice of your time and energy to achieve them. Maybe we do need to address these things, but in the heat of the moment, their relative importance can be significantly overvalued. Emotions also can be guilty of distraction. Fear, anger, and frustration sit atop the list. An equally responsible disruption is our unchecked ego . . . it loves to be stroked, no matter the situation or consequences. If we are to "succeed," we must integrate the immediate events with our larger goals.

Therefore we look for comfort ... something that will stop the emotion, silence the voices, or make our ego proud. In so doing we give away enormous power. Every situation presents the opportunity to further our goals . . . often though, we spend that energy feeding the less important things. Is my need to vent frustration over a repeated mistake in the field (like failing to throw the ball to the cutoff man) more important than Joey's self-confidence or enjoyment of the sport if I scream at him? In the moment I may feel better letting the frustration go, but my longer term goals of being a positive role model, good teacher, and helping the kids grow and enjoy the game may slip away.

A *Reaction* also implies involuntary action — we're just following the laws of physics. Like a billiard ball set in motion, we have little or no control. In *React* mode, we're letting our emotions, frustrations, needs of others and the details of a situation act on us. We appear to be along for the ride, just like the billiard ball with a determined destiny to hit the other balls based on the laws of gravity, geometry, momentum, and motion. When we *React*, free will and choice seem to be distant ideals, far from our reach. Learning to replace *Reaction* with *Response* is like having a remote control billiard ball — we'll still hit some of the other balls, but we get to define the path and have more influence on the outcome.

Respond

A *Response* is a wise, *purposeful* action that balances the perceived urgency or immediate pain/pleasure with larger, more important goals and outcomes.

A *Response* moves us beyond our own narrow slice of the situation and integrates the complexities of people and circumstances. People who *Respond* maintain an unflinching focus on their goals and desired outcomes. A *Response* means that what we say and do should in some way align with, or further, our goals and objectives.

As human beings, we have the ability to transcend our own experience and view a situation from other perspectives. Like a powerful camera, we can zoom in and out, focusing when necessary on small, but perhaps important details. We can also zoom out and get a panoramic view of the whole situation. When we're *Responding*, our zoom button is active, moving back and forth, balancing views of the foreground with the background.

> ***RESPOND***
>
> **A *Response* is a wise, *purposeful* action that balances the perceived urgency or immediate pain/pleasure with larger, more important goals and outcomes.**

However, in *React* mode, the zoom is jammed in full telephoto position, making the wider view much more difficult if not impossible.

React mode is like trying to take a picture of the Grand Canyon with the telephoto lens. You might get some very detailed and interesting shots, but you'd have trouble capturing the size and scope of the place. The many detailed images would have little context without a picture of the whole.

Whether we're aware of it or not, we do have a choice of how we will behave in every situation. We can *React* by taking the course of action that comes first to mind, or is the most familiar, or satisfying or painless. Any of those could be the right thing . . . or each might be the wrong approach . . . but we won't know until we weigh it against our goals.

This difference between *Responding* and *Reacting* is simple to understand, but not always easy to act upon. It requires constant awareness and a lot of practice.

The outcome, however is worth the invested effort. Making *Response* a habit provides coaches a framework to better navigate the choppy waters of youth sports and make good decisions that are in the best interests of their kids — no matter the emotions or pressures of the moment.

React vs. *Respond* is often the difference between being right and being effective. Although we may cling to it until the bitter end (no matter the consequences), being right doesn't always further our goals. Sometimes it can even be a step in the wrong direction. In my effort to convince an umpire I'm right I may unwittingly cross a line and get ejected from a game for arguing. Instead, I may cling to my belief that I'm right but act in a way that preserves the relationship and lobbies for the next close call. Being right is often the narrow slice. Being effective means accomplishing your goals.

Two Major Problems Youth Coaches Face	Tool/Solution
Gap in priorities between what parents and coaches want and what kids want	**Define Fun, Learn, Compete**
Deficiencies in how coaches deal with two types of day-to-day issues. (Strategic decisions & Events of the moment)	**Respond vs. React**

What to Expect . . . Why Read My Journal?

For the last 15 years I've kept a journal as a way to capture and reflect on the things that happen, think about them in different ways, and, hopefully, put them into a more meaningful context. While they are therapeutic to write, I've also found them enjoyable to go back and read at a later date. They help me remember things that happened, see how my thinking has changed over time, and make me wonder how I could have made so many mistakes!

Since the time I became involved in Alan's baseball, I've noticed that more and more of my entries were about kids, teams, and coaching situations. It seems, at least in terms of number of entries, baseball has been a more interesting, if not consuming, part of my life than my trials and tribulations in the workplace and navigating in and around corporate America.

In many ways a journal is a stream of consciousness. Each entry flows as my thoughts focused (or obsessed) around a certain event or issue. I wrote about the hot button of the day to understand it, learn from it, and ultimately purge it from my system. It's the written equivalent of talking to myself, which makes it a little more socially acceptable.

However, taken as a whole, the entries for the baseball season may seem a bit disjointed . . . at least to someone besides me. At one moment I'm ranting about metal bats and the next I'm expressing my concern over which competitive level we'll be placed in. One day I wax poetic about the role of a coach, the next I tumble to the depths of despair when we don't slide at bases, then I share my excitement over a kid's success, and then hop on the shrink's couch and spill my guts about the guilt of being ejected from a game. In this way, a journal is a rare glimpse into the psyche of a coach . . . the thinking isn't linear . . . we're simultaneously considering many different problems, zooming in to the detail of how to best instruct a bunt defense, and then quickly stepping back to wrestle with the philosophical issues of teaching curve balls and the wisdom of having kids play multiple sports.

With that in mind, the journal entries that follow are part story, part essay, part rant, part rambling observation, part confession, and part therapy session. You'll get a primer on dealing with parents and umpires, take a romp down my own memory lane, tackle some of the big issues facing youth sports, and hopefully walk away with a good baseball story that will make you a better coach and parent. You'll get to share some laughs, groan at the frustrations, and wince at the errors, all the while learning some of the lessons I did. And, hopefully, you'll see how to avoid the mistakes I made and you'll finish the book with a better idea of what you want for your kid and your team — and some tangible ideas of how to achieve it.

The entries are from my son Alan's baseball season as a 12-year-old. The stories are true, however some circumstances and all names have been altered to make a point and protect the error-prone. Enjoy!

August 18

What Am I Getting Myself Into?

They say if you want something done right, then do it yourself. That's usually the rationalization of a controlling, never-satisfied perfectionist . . . but I'm beginning to believe it's sage advice for coaching youth sports.

I'm struggling with the decision about where Alan should play baseball next year. He didn't get enough opportunity with the team he played on this season. The two assistant coaches' kids play first and third base and the team was stacked with pitchers, and since he wants to play those positions he's better off on another team. In addition, that team is moving up from the AAA level to majors and I believe Alan would be better off with another season at AAA to gain more knowledge, develop skills, and build confidence. However, there aren't any other existing teams with open slots in our area in his age group. I don't want to drive him to the next town two or three times a week for practices and games, and anyway, he wants to play with his friends.

So that leaves forming my own team as the only other option. That begs the question, "If I do it myself, can I do it right?" Being the head coach is a big responsibility, much larger than the assistant roles I've had over the last six years. Do I want that much accountability? Can I handle all of the duties?

I suppose I have come a long way as a coach. Here I am considering taking on the head coaching responsibilities for a team of 12-year-olds next spring, and it was just seven years ago I was petrified by the thought of coaching Alan's team. I remember it well . . .

. . . I was getting myself a piece of toast in the kitchen one morning while Bev fed the kids. In between bites we reviewed the day ahead.

"And then after lunch I'll register Alan for soccer," said Bev. Alan let out a whoop as he stirred his oatmeal. My four-year-old was itching to play soccer this fall in what would be his first youth sports experience.

I exhaled a deep sigh and rolled my eyes, mentally covering familiar ground. "I just don't like the game. It's such a waste of your hands," I complained for the umpteenth time. Bev quickly gave me her "not now" look — a stern reminder not to ruin the game of soccer for Alan.

Despite the warning I continued, "I played it once when I was nine . . ."

"Yeah, you were awful, you didn't understand the game," she interrupted, cutting short the discussion-soon-to-become-argument while pouring juice for Alan and Rachel. "All you did was run around and nobody ever passed you the ball. They wouldn't let you play goalie, which you thought was a tragedy because it was the only position that let you use your hands. So you quit after just one humiliating season." Her rapid cadence and dismissive tone bordered on condescension.

Defeated, I changed the subject. "Well, I can't wait for him to get interested in baseball next spring. Isn't that right, buddy?" I asked, messing up his hair.

Later that afternoon I got a call at work from Bev. "Hi, hon. What's up? You got Alan registered for soccer?"

Silence.

"Well, there was a problem," she began slowly. "The league was filled. I don't know how it happened so quickly, but all of the teams were full."

She let the likelihood of a disappointed four-year-old hang in the air for a few moments. Just as I started to shift into problem-solving mode, she said, "But I talked to the guy running the league and after offering him something I was able to get him on a team."

My mind raced with what sort of bargain she had to strike with this guy.

Before I could guess, she explained, "They were short of coaches. So, in exchange for adding one more kid, you get to coach his team."

Silence.

Finally she broke the quiet. "Don't you think Alan will be happy?" she asked, knowing I wouldn't fall for the misdirection.

Alan was millions of miles away in my mind at that moment. Yeah, okay, hooray for the kid. But, more importantly, what about me? I'M the coach? I'm the COACH? I've never coached before. My dad was my baseball coach growing up, but that genealogy and perhaps an old dusty plastic whistle squirreled away in a drawer were about all the qualifications I could muster at that point. And wait, didn't Bev understand that I played soccer once when I was nine, hated it, and still don't understand the game?

"You'll be great," she pronounced, closing the sell. "See you at home, soccer coach Dan." With this syrupy-sweet touch of sarcasm, she hung up.

I sat in my office with the phone still in hand, staring blankly at the wall, the gravity of my situation slowly sinking in . . . coach Dan . . . soccer coach Dan . . .

And thus began my coaching career.

I've come a long way in those seven years. I'm still not a big fan of soccer, but I now enjoy working with kids, seeing them learn, grow, and have fun. It's a thrill to teach them something new and watch them tinker with the concept, have some initial success, and eventually make it their own.

I used to be intimidated by the sets of 11 eyes staring up at me when we'd ask them to huddle up. I was afraid everything I would say would come across as pithy, or worse, would be so boring, off-base, or over the head of the kids I was trying to help. It's not always easy to connect with kids and get your message to resonate. They can be a tough crowd, and once lost, they are difficult to get back.

Now I get those same sets of eyes looking at me and I see that they are simply hungry. They have an almost insatiable appetite for fun; they're starving for new things to make them competitive. Yeah, I'm still capable of saying some really stupid things, or even worse, being at a loss for words. But I've grown to be comfortable in who I am as a coach, what I have to offer and accept the fact that I too will make mistakes. Maybe, most importantly, I've realized that, if I own the miscues, they're okay. The kids are much better at forgiving than the adults, although the older they get, the less forgetting and more razzing they seem to do . . .

I'm still on the fence, but getting closer to talking myself into coaching a team of my own next year. I'll sleep on it a few more nights and make a final decision next week.

August 23

Deciding to Coach

I've decided to be the head coach of Alan's team next season. I'm excited to share my knowledge, leverage my organizational skills, and pass on my passion for the game. Although I've been an assistant coach for the last six years, this is a big jump in responsibility because the head coach is accountable for everything.

A smooth operation requires me to manage the finances, organize parent meetings, register for tournaments, coordinate logistics with the league, order uniforms, schedule fields and practices, get team insurance, collect birth certificates, fund raise, coordinate team photos, purchase equipment, etc.

Managing the parents and keeping any potential issues from showing up on the field or souring the stands will be no small task, requiring a significant time commitment to communicate with everyone as needed. In addition, I need to develop an overall strategy for the team, continually assess talent, and build a plan for each practice that includes drills and activities appropriate to our needs at the time. This means I'll need to brush up on my knowledge and instructional content for all of the positions. I'll have assistant coaches Robert and Sam lead on different areas, but I still need to know a lot more than I do now. Finally,

I'll have a big handful of game day responsibilities, including making the lineup and the pressures of making the right decisions on the field. Wow! Listing it all in one spot like this shows it is a very big job!

The rewards, though, will be the smiles and satisfaction of the kids. I have helped create a lot of those over the years as an assistant, but as head coach I'll get to set the direction that will make it easier for me to have the impact I'd like to. I'm excited by the opportunity and the challenge.

I'm going to keep a journal this season so I can keep track of what I'm learning, analyze and reflect upon events as they happen, and create a record of what we did that I can review with pride and a smile when I'm older and grayer . . . let the games begin!!

August 25

My Most Rewarding Baseball Moments

I'm happy with my decision to coach next season. It feels right and I'm excited to start pulling the team together. The process of determining why I want to coach, what I have to offer, and what I want to accomplish opened a floodgate of memories. It made me realize I should take a moment and give thanks: I've been extremely fortunate. Not only did I have success with baseball, but more important, I also had loads of fun.

Baseball is intertwined with many of my childhood memories. During non-school waking hours I was usually in a game, practicing, or playing on a makeshift diamond in the driveway with the neighborhood kids. When there weren't enough friends around to field a team, I was playing catch, re-sorting my baseball cards, inventing a wiffle ball game with Dad, reading about baseball, or playing the ageless "Strat-o-matic" game with my friend Shaun. Baseball was central to just about everything I did from age five to 20. I formed a tremendous relationship with the game that continues to this day. Deserving of the credit are the many coaches, parents, teammates, and opponents I encountered over the years.

With this background, I undertake this responsibility of being the head coach next season very seriously. I have the opportunity to fuel the kids' passion for the game, teach them about baseball, make them better players and better people, and have fun. I'll be helping create another generation of baseball memories.

As I time-travel back three decades and brush away the cobwebs surrounding my memory, a few rewarding moments are worth writing down.

Steve Kuster

I hit my very first over-the-fence homerun the summer after sixth grade. Making it more special was that I hit it off Steve Kuster, one of the best pitchers in the league. All through grade school Steve had been my rival. We never had class together, but we always battled every recess at the sport in season.

The night I hit the homerun we played at one of the nicer fields in the county. The diamond was carved into a grove of cottonwoods near a creek at the bottom of a small bluff. While the dimensions were similar to other fields, the hill along two sides of the field and the cottonwoods surrounding the others gave it a very cozy feel.

Steve threw hard and was, what I call, effectively wild. He had a reputation for hitting batters and most of us were afraid to dig in against him. It was the top of the first inning and, in typical fashion, Steve struck out the first batter and walked the next. Tom sat on our bench angry that he had swung and missed while Ben stood on first base glad that ball four hadn't hit him in the ribs.

I remember being uncharacteristically relaxed as I stood in the batter's box and took a few practice swings. Steve's first pitch was a bullet right down the middle. I took a sweet natural swing and hit it squarely. The ball jumped off my wood bat on a high arc. I'd never seen a ball fly like that from the vantage of the batter's box. The left fielder ran back but soon gave up and watched it disappear about 20 feet beyond the fence into the brush and fallen logs at the base of the cottonwoods.

I was completely surprised. "I just hit a homerun!" I thought to myself. Running the bases in this situation was a new experience, and for a brief moment I wasn't sure what I was supposed to do. Fortunately, there's very little magic to it . . . run towards first base and keep turning left . . .

The reality didn't set in until I neared second base and Steve was smiling and shaking his head — nobody had ever hit one off of him. He wasn't mad; just surprised like me.

"I hit that off of Steve Kuster," I told myself, growing more and more proud. The shortstop and third baseman each raised their hands and gave me high fives as I trotted by.

As I neared home plate Steve smiled and said, "Nice hit, Dan."

I remember saying, "Thanks," and shrugging my shoulders with a disbelieving smile. Both of us were simply enjoying the novelty of the moment.

My teammates congratulated me at home plate and escorted me back to the bench. I only hit three more homeruns in the remaining eight years of my career . . . but few baseball memories are as special as beating Steve Kuster in that one at-bat.

Gary's Slide

One night Gary Mumford came barreling around third base on his way to score in a close game. Not blessed with speed, we knew Gary was going to make it a very close play at the plate. The throw from the outfielder was accurate and arrived ahead of Gary. But for some reason (which he couldn't explain later), he dove headfirst and his fully outstretched hand brushed the side of the plate. In the dust and confusion, the ball squirted away from the catcher and Gary was safe.

Back in the mid- and late-1970s Pete Rose was one of the few ballplayers who slid headfirst into a base. That practice didn't become popular until the 1980s with the likes of Ricky Henderson and Tim Raines.

Gary came back into the dugout breathing hard, covered in powdery dirt with scrapes on his elbow and hand. We were all happy that he scored but we were more entertained by his slide and started calling him "Mr. Rose."

Ben walked over to him and said, "Mr. Rose, can I have your autograph?"

Gary, bent over and still brushing the dust off his socks, said, without looking up, "Get away kid, I'm busy."

We laughed about that for several more innings.

"Get away kid, I'm busy," became our catch phrase for just about everything for the rest of the season.

My Only No-Hitter

It was the summer after seventh grade and we were playing in the semi-finals of the league championship. A win and we played the following weekend for the big trophy.

I was pitching well that night, although I was a bit wild and walked five batters. I didn't realize I had a no-hitter going, even in the sixth inning when we were ahead 5 - 0. I walked the first batter and he was still on first base with one out.

The next batter hit a ground ball to Tom at shortstop, who flipped it to Ben at second base, who made a quick pivot and strong throw to first for a game-ending double play. We were excited, not so much by the win, but it was the first time any of us had turned a double play in the infield ... ever. We felt we had arrived ... kids don't turn double plays . . . big leaguers turn double plays!

We were jumping up and down, thrilled with the accomplishment as well as with the opportunity to play for the championship. I discovered later that night while looking through the scorebook that I had thrown a no-hitter. Nobody knew or cared . . . we were celebrating!

The funny thing is that I remember we did win the championship the next weekend, but to this day I recall nothing about that game. I can't say who we played, what field it was on, what the score was, or if I had a hit. My memory is the semi-final and Ben jumping up and down after making his throw to first for the double play. I vividly remember all of us huddling near first base, smiling, yelling, and laughing.

I guess you never know what will have the most impact on kids . . .

And the more I reflect on my own memories, it is not the winning and losing that sticks out. It's the funny plays, the friendships, the lessons learned, and the colorful characters. Wins and losses hold no lasting value . . . what really counts when you begin to add things up — at the end of the season, or when you're 42-years-old — are the jokes, broken bats, forgotten gloves, thrills of competition, great catches, bad hops that left stitch marks on my collar bone, that Ben always wore a Cincinnati Reds jacket, the satisfaction of driving a pitch back up the middle, Mark White breaking his nose on a foul ball, striking out Jerry Thompson on a curve ball the first time I learned how to throw it, bloody knees from poor slides at second, continually refining my batting stance to look like a right-handed George Brett, laughing in the dugout . . .

These are the catalysts for the learning that takes place and are the heart of what makes the game of baseball time well spent.

As I thought back at these good times, I couldn't say what our win-loss record was in any of our seasons, I couldn't say how many hits I had or how many batters I struck out on the mound.

But I ***can*** say that I had success and I had fun.

That's why today when someone says "youth baseball," or starts talking about their own experiences, I immediately get a warm feeling in my chest and crack a smile. I'm not thinking of anything in particular. In fact, I'm not even thinking yet. It's an involuntary response. Deep down inside my psyche I carry the knowledge, belief, and/or experience that baseball is, has been, and always will be fun. That's what bubbles up, unconsciously at first, and quickly gets me charged up to play … and now coach.

My challenge this season will be to help create similar experiences for the 11 kids on my team. I want them to have equally rewarding experiences. I want them to have as much fun as I did. I want them to learn what I learned. I want them to have the passion for the game that I do. I want them to want to coach their kids when they are my age, and I want them to have a good role model to draw from. I want every kid to get a bunch of his own fond memories this season.

August 28

Forming a Team … Getting My Head Straight

I've been doing a lot of thinking about the team next season and there's a lot more to it than finding 11 kids who will play for me. Getting things right up front as I form the team is crucial to having success and fun next season. Here's what I'm thinking.

Many parents and coaches believe that you start putting a baseball team together by having a tryout. Secure a field, set a date, spread the word and hope you attract a few ringers. On the big day, line up the kids at shortstop hit ground balls, observe their form with the glove, and judge the strength and accuracy of their throw to first base. Put them in the outfield and watch how they gauge fly balls, see if they are moving forward on the catch, and if they can hit a cutoff man and throw to a base. Give each of them 10 to15 cuts at the plate and look for bat speed, aggressiveness, and the ability to drive the ball. Then take the kids who want to pitch and put them in the bullpen. Make note of how hard each one throws, wince at their mechanics, and determine if they can get it close to the plate.

Yes, for many of us, this is how we begin putting a team together. However, I believe to have a productive season, a successful coach will start at a more foundational level.

Back up several steps.

We have to first get our heads straight. We have to be very clear on a number of things before we begin our jobs as General Manager and do the recruiting, horse trading, and herd-thinning required to put a team together. Before all of that, we have to answer two fundamental questions:

1. *Why do I want to coach?*
2. *What are we going to accomplish?*

To answer each of these a coach needs to do a healthy amount of soul searching, think about his situation from many different perspectives, and have several good conversations with significant others . . . this includes his son, spouse, and prospective assistant coaches. He can't simply answer, "Because I did it last year and we want to win." Not good enough. Face it . . . we're going to spend four to six months doing it . . . we owe the kids, parents, and ourselves more than that.

The following are my answers, which are based on several days of thought, discussion, and reflection.

Why Do I Want to Coach?

I have something to offer. That's the shortest and most accurate answer, and the one I gave the committee that interviewed and selected coaches for our league. I acquired a specialized knowledge of the game over 15 consecutive springs and summers. It began when I learned to hit the ball off the tee and ground to a halt my sophomore year in college with the third surgery on my pitching shoulder. In that decade and a half I played roughly 600 games, learning fundamentals, tips, techniques, skills, and strategies from nearly 40 coaches and their assistants.

I earned all-state honors in both my junior and senior years in high school, went to a major conference Division I university on scholarship, and competed with or against roughly 20 guys who played some level of professional baseball.

This is not to say that all youth sports coaches should have played in college. I know many college and pro athletes who make terrible youth coaches because they can't teach, can't relate to kids, or most tragically, their egos get in the way. They struggle to translate and convey the methods they've learned or the things they've done naturally without instruction. On the flip side, many great youth coaches never played beyond high school. To be credible and technically competent, they attend clinics, read books, watch videos, and learn from other coaches and experts.

The point is that I believe I have something unique and valuable to share with the kids . . . good coaches know what their strengths are and what they can offer. They leverage these throughout the season and, where they have gaps in knowledge or expertise, they get an assistant or volunteer to help.

In addition, I still play the game. Every Sunday between April and September when Alan doesn't have a game I lace up the cleats, grab my glove, and play in a competitive adult baseball league. This enables me to use the fundamentals I learned long ago. More accurately, it gives me the ***opportunity*** to do so . . . sometimes the mind is willing but the body is no longer capable! Beyond this thrill of competition the 35-and-over league brings, it is relevant to the coaching question because I am still learning, engaged in the effort to execute plays, and I can better empathize when kids make mistakes. I too, continue to make errors which reminds me how difficult it is to play the game well . . . consistently.

Finally, my penchant for weekly embarrassment demonstrates that I still have a deep passion for the game. Giving young players a taste of this passion, and helping ignite and fuel theirs, are probably the biggest and best things I bring to the table. I absolutely love the game of baseball. I love all it has to offer. I love the opportunity it brings to have fun, to learn, and to compete. I want the kids who play for me to feel that too.

I want them to enjoy standing on the pitchers mound with a slight breeze blowing the snow in their face. I want them to love that their undershirts get drenched with sweat on a hot summer afternoon while playing shortstop. I want them to ache for the opportunity to come to the plate with two outs and the go-ahead run on second base. I want them dreaming about how high they'll jump after striking out the cleanup hitter with a full count and the bases loaded, ahead by one run in the bottom of the last inning.

Knowledge, experience, and passion are what I bring to the table. I also have a strong sense of organization, process, and structure that makes for a smooth baseball operation and maintains the focus on the field, not bungled logistical details. Orchestrating the paperwork, scheduling, coordinating with the league, planning practices, dealing with parents and organizing the logistics for travel and tournaments are all strengths of mine (although I readily admit that I'd much rather be on the field with the kids than working through the administrative stuff!).

And there's also a personal agenda that benefits everyone who plays for me. I want to coach because I want to create the right environment for Alan. Every parent wants that for his or her kid and coaches are no exception. Last season was a tough one for him. I was the pitching coach on his team and unfortunately there wasn't enough encouragement or sufficient opportunity to play the positions he's good at (or could be, given the chance). He joined a team with nine core players and the positions were mostly set. This year he needs a situation where he gets to play a lot, have fun, enjoy success, and build his confidence. He needs the opportunity to play with friends (old and new) and learn the next layer of fundamentals.

I believe there are a lot of kids in a similar situation . . . if the environment I create is good for Alan, it will be good for them too.

Another motivator for me is that I feel a certain sense of civic duty to repay the coaches who toiled in the sun and snow for me all of those years. My dad and his assistant coaches as well as those in high school, American Legion, and college gave a lot to me. Paying it forward . . . that's how the game of baseball remains strong from generation to generation.

Finally, it's important to recognize that I can't be 100 percent altruistic in my motives for wanting to coach. Obviously I have to personally get something out of it. If I don't, then I won't have the energy and enthusiasm necessary to engage the hearts and minds of 12-year-olds day-in and day-out for the entire season. But my personal motives MUST center on helping kids learn, sharing expertise, and the sense of accomplishment that comes with bringing joy to others.

If I'm motivated solely by a desire to win, build a program, be in charge, be recognized as a great coach, etc., then I should spare the kids, parents and league the hassle. Everyone would be better off if I simply joined a fantasy baseball league. If I'm focused on my own ego first, which by the way, may be difficult for me to recognize on my own, I'm going to be frustrated and the other adults will despise me.

So, honestly, what do I hope to personally gain from this coaching experience, beyond knowledge transfer and paying it forward? I enjoy the problem-solving challenge of getting individuals to perform at their best and molding their contributions into a successful team. I do this for a living with adults in the workplace, but kids present a different challenge. It's an undertaking I'm excited about!

I also want the sense of satisfaction that comes with helping each player grow and learn. I want kids to look back on the seasons they played for me as good times. Hopefully, 20 years from now when they hear my name they will smile.

What Are We Going to Accomplish?

Youth sports would be a different place if all coaches and parents asked themselves this question, gave it some good, ego-penetrating thought . . . and then, and only then, answered honestly to themselves . . . and each other. All too often they don't. Or they don't adequately define their terms. As a result, at various times throughout the season, major conflicts erupt because of differing expectations.

For example, how should a coach reconcile the following conflicting needs? Jimmy and his parents want, and expect, to win every game, while Jeffery and his parents just want him to play and have fun. Joey's parents want him to be a power hitter and play in high school . . . but Joey isn't all that interested in baseball, he just wants to have fun spending time with his two best friends who are stars on the team. Karl the assistant coach wants to build a dynasty and win the league championship with this team the next two seasons before the kids enter high school, while Larry, the other assistant, wants his son to move up to a higher competitive level next year. Each of these things is possible . . . however, achieving them all, with the same team and group of parents in the same season, probably isn't.

Talking about it in general terms doesn't hack it either. Parents, coaches, and players each can read different things into the same word or phrase. "We're going to be a very competitive team this season," sounds like a pretty good thing to most of us. But what does that really mean? Is a 9 - 9 record competitive? Is 5 - 13 competitive if 10 of the losses were by one run? What about 14 - 4? 18 - 0? Many parents equate "competitive" with "winning" . . . do I? Why or why not?

I also hear the phrase, "We're going to give every kid a chance to play the positions he wants this season." Sounds great! Sign me up.

Um, hold on.

Wait a minute . . . is that for the whole season? What if the kid has no talent whatsoever to play a position he wants (like pitcher)? Is he still going to get the opportunity? Is it an equal opportunity? For an equal number of innings? Really? How will I explain that to the parents of the best pitcher on the team? How about to the kid who can barely get it to the plate? I must choose my answers carefully . . . those parents don't care about winning, just that their kid can play. And I might have to be explaining these things to parents while cleaning up the dugout after a tough 8 - 7 loss. I must be aware that my answers are public information . . . the parents of the best player are huddled only 30 feet away, listening to every word. It is better to have thought this through while I'm putting the team together in the fall than at the spur of the moment in May when the parents are staring at me waiting for an intelligent answer.

As I sipped a cup of coffee early one morning a couple of days ago, I realized the questions will get more complicated as the season unfolds and the path I've defined resonates with some and repulses others:

- If the assistant coach's kid plays third base will other kids get an equal opportunity?

- If we lose our first five games will every kid still get the chance to play where he wants?
- What if we win the first five?
- What if Jimmy makes seven errors at shortstop in the first six games . . .
- Does Johnny get to play more innings there?
- How will I split that playing time?
- Will I simply rotate game-to-game or inning-to-inning?
- What if it is Jimmy's turn against the best team in the league and, instead, I put him in the outfield so we have a better chance of winning?
- What if it is his turn in the sixth inning of a tie game?
- What if Jimmy's family have been close friends since the kids were five years old? What if Johnny's have been too?
- Am I ready to defend those decisions to Jimmy, Johnny, and their parents when they're waiting for me outside the dugout after the game?
- How would my answers be similar or different if I were coaching nine-year-olds rather than 12-year-olds?

My head was spinning and my stomach was turning as I pondered these questions . . . I suppose that means I'm giving it the proper amount of thought. Getting everyone onboard isn't going to be easy. Keeping them on the boat will be downright difficult. And, I'm sure there will be times that going down with the ship will seem both unavoidable and attractive.

I need to crystallize this thinking and put it in writing before I finalize the roster. This should ensure that, at least in the beginning, we all have a clear understanding of what we were going to accomplish and how we'll do it. This will be especially important for my team because I don't have a core group returning … I'm essentially starting from scratch. I have Alan and the sons of two assistant coaches on the roster; we'll recruit the other eight players.

Here are my three priorities for the team:

Fun, Learn, Compete

These will guide our decisions throughout the season. Together they form the backbone of our team's vision — a critical element in leading any group to success. But, obviously, these terms can mean something different to everyone depending on the age and ability of the kids, as well as on the desires of the parents and coaches. Here the definitions I'll give the parents of my 12-year-olds.

1. ***Have Fun.*** These are the golden years of youth baseball. The kids should love playing and it should, above all else, be fun. If they're not having fun, we are doing something terribly wrong as coaches and parents. While practices may be grueling, failure frustrating, and the weather miserable, on the whole, kids should enjoy their time on the field and the nine-month journey with teammates. When we have fun with an activity, we are much more likely to learn, have confidence, develop, make friends, do our best, etc. And, if the kids have fun, they will want to continue to play the game next season and beyond. We'll be giving them the experiences and memories that will last them a lifetime. Few will look back on this season when they are 30 years old and remember our final win-loss record . . . but when the subject of baseball comes up 20 years from

now, the smile on their faces will reveal, without a doubt, that it was a fun experience.

2. ***Learn.*** Player development will be critical this year, as they will have the skills, attention spans, and desire to learn more strategy and the finer fundamentals of the game. There is a tremendous amount we can teach them about the game . . . some of this will help them learn about themselves and what type of person they can become. How they deal with failure, adversity, success, etc. teaches them valuable lessons they will apply throughout their lives. The coaches will provide instruction and the opportunity to apply it in practice and game situations. We are more concerned about the kids learning the proper fundamentals than the final win-loss record.

3. ***Compete.*** Our objective is to be competitive in everything we do, not winning at all costs. This is true both as individuals as well as a team. The best growth occurs against equal or slightly better competition. We have more fun when the game is on the line and the outcome in doubt. To get better, you have to play against better competition and this means we will lose some games. It's also important to recognize that winning is different than being competitive. Beating a team 15 - 2 isn't competitive for anyone, and little learning/growth occurs. It's usually not much fun either. The kids should want to win and give 100 percent effort to achieve it, however, they shouldn't feel intense pressure to win from parents and coaches. While we want the kids to enjoy the thrill of winning (and the sense of accomplishment that comes with it), a team that finishes the season 10 - 8 often learns a lot more, collectively and individually, than the 17 - 1 team that wins most games by run rule.

Although we'll be playing in a competitive division, it is important that we try to give equal playing time as long as the kids give 100 percent effort and display a good attitude. However, poor attitude and lackluster effort will earn a kid time on the bench. This at times might make it difficult to be competitive, and I realize it will probably cost us a few wins here and there. However given Alan's experience last year, it is okay for the pendulum swing away from winning back towards fun and opportunity.

Equal playing time won't work for every coach or every team, nor should it. And my approach may change next year even if most of the team stays intact . . . kids grow and develop and their needs change quickly. As they get older and rise to higher levels of competition, the expectations become more demanding and playing time is often a reward, not an inalienable right. But that's a decision every coach and group of parents needs to make . . . before the season begins.

I also realize that given the remaining talent in our area that isn't already on a team, we are not likely to be a powerhouse. We'll compete and win our share of games, but we're not going to be an elite team.

I'm fine with that. Really. I'd like for Alan to have the opportunity to play in high school and perhaps beyond. Maybe he'll get that chance; maybe he won't. But predicting if he will have the ability and desire five years from now is nearly impossible. "If he keeps progressing at the same rate, he'll have a shot," you think . . . the truth is, progress never follows a predictable curve. It comes in waves and batches, ebbing and flowing throughout their pre-teen and teenage years. You don't know when they'll hit their eventual ceiling until it happens. Some bump it hard at 13. Others peak at 17 or 18. Some hit it at age seven and have been slowly sliding since. Others keep it going into their 30s or even 40s.

The point is you can't predict that when they are 11. Tarot and palm reading give more and better insight into future success at this age.

However, I can rule kids out at this age ... not so much on ability but on desire. If Alan is in a situation that isn't fun and he isn't learning, he'll lose interest and won't want to continue to play. That's a sure-fire way to prevent a college scholarship. He'll find another sport or activity that brings more satisfaction. I will be okay with that if that is his true interest or passion. It will be a tragedy, though, if that happened because I pushed too hard as a parent/coach or put him in a situation that was wrong for his needs.

The **Fun, Learn, Compete** framework is very flexible. A coach can define each at the beginning of the season to match the needs, priorities, and goals of his group of kids and parents. Is a priority to prepare them for the high school game? Put that in the definition of **Learn**. As nine-year-olds do you want them to play with their core group of fiends? Include that in the **Fun** section. Want to win more? Augment your definition of **Compete**. The point is that the coach can define these any way he wants . . . they just need to be clear, understood, and shared.

I like my definitions. They fit what Alan needs and they align with my coaching style. This exercise got my head straight and positions me to recruit 10 like-minded families. Now, with the help of my assistant coaches Sam and Robert, I have to go find them!

A Concern

I hope I'm doing the right thing. Kaleb, the son of my assistant coach Robert, is a terrific kid. He's mature for his age, has a great sense of humor, and always tries hard. But he's not yet shown the speed, coordination, or fine motor skills that the other kids on the team have. He's going to have to stretch and improve significantly to play at this competitive level.

As I think about what we're trying to achieve as individuals and a team — **Fun, Learn, Compete** — I have no doubts Kaleb will be fine on the first two. He knows how to have fun, and his laugh is contagious. He's also willing to try new things and listens as well as any 12-year-old. But I'm not convinced he can compete at the AAA level. Fun, learn, compete is a three-legged stool . . . all three have to be there or things quickly fall down. Being overmatched takes the fun out of the experience. And if it becomes obvious to the team it could be tough on him — I don't want to put anyone in a position of being thought of as the weakest link. At this age so much of a player's self-esteem is tied to what they do athletically.

Right now Kaleb is behind. But he's determined to play at this level and he's asking for the opportunity. And, Robert seems convinced this is the right move for Kaleb. It will be fun to coach with Robert again because we've had many good times coaching together in years past. I'd like to believe Kaleb's hard work and determination will pay off ... over the long haul, that's what baseball rewards.

Kaleb and I decided to give it a try.

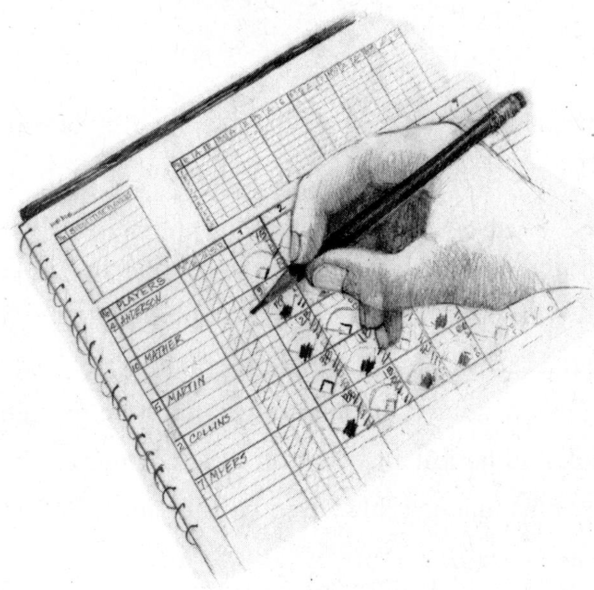

September 10

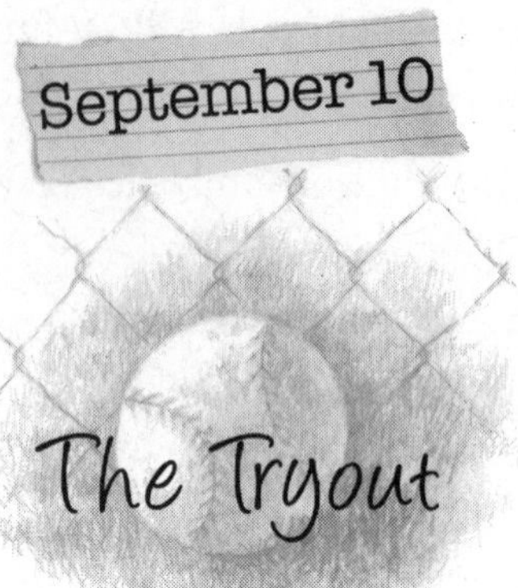

The Tryout

I was thrilled to stay just a half-step behind everyone at the tryout yesterday afternoon. All-in-all it went okay for my first attempt at organizing one of these assessments, but I underestimated the amount of orchestration and thought required to support the process flow. It may have looked fine to the participating families, but to me it never felt easy, comfortable, or the way I thought it would. I imagined a clipboard in hand, calmly making notes about each player that would magically develop into a numerical analysis of the perfect four or five players to select. Maybe that happens in Hollywood; but not in Denver . . . at least not yesterday.

I got to the field 20 minutes early to set up. I had registration forms, stickers with numbers on them, a box of pens, several evaluation sheets full of columns of numbers aching to be circled, a bucket of balls, bases, a pitching rubber, my glove, and my wood fungo bat. I'm sure I resembled a miner's pack mule as I gathered up this pile of gear in the parking lot. It was quite a load. As I slammed the trunk closed, I met my first participant and his dad. So much for the head start.

The dad started talking and, frankly, wouldn't shut up. Empty-handed, he watched me juggle the equipment load, never offering to carry anything on the 150-yard march to the field. He told me his hitting philosophy and which pro players also used that strategy. He gave me the behind-the-scenes tour of three camps his son had been to in the last six months, providing dirt on at least one major leaguer. I think I only got in two or three words by the time we got to the field, and the chatter box kept talking as I started to set things up. He was oblivious to every non-verbal and verbal cue I was sending: shut up and let me get organized!

Seemingly unaware that I would soon have at least 25 kids and parents descending on the field expecting order and instructions, he proceeded to tell me what a tremendous athlete his son was. Hands down he was the best player on his previous team. Dad wasn't sure if it was this kid's exceptional talent or his own expertise as a pitching coach that now enabled this 11-year-old to throw a devastating curve ball. Apparently a former pro-player had seen him pitch and was convinced that he has a real shot at playing college ball. Tragically, the only devastation I could envision coming from the curve ball of any 11-year-old was going to be the poor kid's shoulder and elbow by the time he turns 15. College ball is a long, long way off if you can't straighten your arm.

I put down my bag and the bucket of balls and began to make piles of the registration forms, numbers, pens and other materials we'd soon need. Dad, meanwhile, continued the monologue, describing in detail the five awful things about his previous coach and why they decided to leave the team. I was about to gnaw off a limb to get away from this guy when coaches Robert and Sam unwittingly came to my rescue; I was elated to introduce the three of them and quickly escape to the other side of the fence to finish setting up. Sam kept shooting me, "What did I ever do to you?" looks, but at least one of us was free.

Despite the pain of this conversation, I realized my job was already a little easier . . . I had just made a decision on one of the 25 kids.

Thanks but no thanks, dad. I didn't even need to see the kid put on his glove to know that this wasn't going to work. Nothing I did would be good enough for dad. No matter how much we might talk about equal playing time, the first occasion his son sat his rotation on the bench I'd get a visit from the stands. The ensuing conversation would, by comparison, make this one seem pleasant. It's better to weed this out immediately than try to maneuver the other 10 kids around this landmine.

In the nick of time I got registration process flowing and had each family complete a one-page questionnaire asking about their goals for the upcoming season. Some of my more hardened, old-school coaching colleagues might have considered it a bit dorky, but I'm realizing it is difficult to pin down people on their priorities. I've talked to about 30 different parents and coaches in the last three weeks, and left to their own devices, adults are all over the map in terms of what they want from a youth baseball experience, what they value, what they expect from a coach, and what they're willing to sacrifice to make it all work.

I'm also realizing that people define terms very differently. To some, competitive and winning are synonymous, while others see them as completely different ideas. Some rationalize winning by saying that it's a lot more fun to win than it is to lose, therefore if you focus on winning, you kill two birds with one stone. Most haven't thought much about any of these issues in any depth, and will, like lemmings, nod their heads in apparent agreement with whoever is talking.

To make families draw their own lines in the sand, I asked the following open-ended questions on the flip side of the registration form:

- It will be a successful season if . . .
- I/we will be disappointed at the end of next season if . . .

I also had them rank their top three priorities from these six:

- Winning
- Playing with your current friends
- Learning the game
- Having fun
- Playing at the highest level possible
- Being competitive

As the parents and kids worked through these answers, each kid applied one of the large stickers to his chest with a number between 1 and 30 on it so we could easily identify him on the field. I felt a little like a clerk at a governmental agency, processing paperwork and trying to keep things organized, but fortunately Robert and Sam were there to help and get the kids warmed up. This was turning out to be an excellent process . . . until a gust blew half of my forms and stickers across the diamond. I'm no gazelle to begin with, but there's just no graceful or dignified way to chase paper in the wind.

Eventually we found a rhythm, Sam and Robert hitting balls while they made mental notes and I wrote down what I saw. But it was difficult to quickly refer back and forth to my list of player numbers and rate them on their performance. By the time we were done with a certain drill and had the timing and sequencing figured out, it was on to the next one. After 15 minutes I ditched my numerical rating system in favor of three columns: yes, no and maybe. That simplified my world and the goal became to move the "maybes" into one of the other columns based on what I saw.

About 30 minutes into the tryout I discovered there was a set of identical twins. They were sporting their uniforms from the previous season, and obviously, had the same name stitched on the back. The only way I could tell them apart was the numbers 34 and 36 on the back . . . close enough to confuse the heck out of me! I was panicked! I couldn't tell which was which! They somehow slipped through a flaw in my registration process. I struggled for about 10 minutes, missing a whole group of kids catching fly balls while trying to sort it out. I was then hit with a blinding glimpse of the obvious . . . it really didn't matter . . . I'm sure their parents considered the kids a package deal. I couldn't offer just one a spot on the team . . . duh!

Near the end of the tryout I had one kid inform me very matter-of-factly that he would by far be the best player on the team. He proceeded to tell me what the other kids were doing wrong and why he was a better player as he shagged balls in left field and we watched others take batting practice. He had talent, but sadly, I saw that he wouldn't be fun to be around — for me or the other kids. Nope . . . wasn't going to work. I don't need that dynamic on my team, even if he was the second coming of Babe Ruth.

Ultimately Sam, Robert, and I got a good look at 25 kids who love baseball and just want to play. We saw some kids who have talent and others that have relied solely on their passion for the game to get them this far. Hats off to both groups and all in between. A tryout is a scary thing. There's nowhere to hide and it's difficult to soften the sting of not making the cut. We realized there's plenty of talent to choose from and there will be enough kids to form at least one other team.

Although it was stressful to organize, the energy, excitement, and hope of a tryout is a pretty cool thing. Until, that is, you have to start making choices and explain your decisions to parents . . .

Sam, Robert and I will get together tonight to select the team.

September 14

Selecting the Team — Who Will Go With Us?

I'm already feeling the weight of being the head coach. Selecting the team hasn't been an easy job. I feel tremendous responsibility picking who will come with us and who will not. In a sometimes-not-so-small way, I'm making decisions that will impact kids and families for the rest of their lives.

That sounds a bit self-important, I'll admit. It's not that if the kids don't play for me they'll have a miserable season, lead to a horrible childhood, eventually culminating in a life of crime and despair.

I don't mean that.

I am, though, charged with accurately assessing a kid's ability, personality, desires, and family situation and making a sound decision if my team is a good spot for him. If I assess and choose wisely, then the kid's passion for the game has the best chance to grow. If I screw up, though, the kid may struggle in this team environment, and I run the risk of creating a less enjoyable experience for the other 10 players and families.

And for me as the coach, creating a team has ramifications far beyond the playing field because I invite the kids and families into my house everyday. Not physically, but intellectually and emotionally. We don't cohabitate, but I do live with them. Whenever there's a practice, a game, or a team issue I'm wrestling with, I bring them into my house. If I'm upset with a parent, I'm likely to discuss the problem with Bev, which takes me away from my family just as if the person had dropped by and sat in my living room for 30 minutes. Is that how I'd want to spend my time?

Because I'm making the decisions, I need to be very clear . . . is this somebody that I could get along with? I need to feel these are people I enjoy being around and will problem-solve with me when issues arise. It doesn't mean we'd have to be best buds, but philosophically we must be in alignment with what we want for the kids and from the team experience.

This is why I felt the questionnaire was important. Yeah, people could fudge and put down what they thought I wanted to see, but it was a starting point and I really did pay attention to what people wrote. In addition, I was able to tell a lot about a kid and the family by watching them interact before, during, and after the tryout. What they talk about, what instructions the parents give, and how they treat each other are clues. If the kid is constantly looking into the stands, hoping for acceptance and direction, that's a warning sign.

I also believe that my intuition gives me important information. Some of the best advice I ever received about personnel decisions was from a boss who told me to simply trust my gut. He explained that I should read the resumes, conduct the interviews, and check the references, "Be thorough and leave no stone unturned," he counseled.

Then, he said, when it was time to make the decision, "You have to trust your gut . . . visualize the person being on your team. Think about everything you know about them, their personality, mannerisms, what they said in the interview, and how they said it. Then see what your gut says." To do that, he explained, you just have to ask yourself one question, "Are you going to be excited when they walk through the door Monday morning, or are you going to be holding your breath?"

This advice has served me well in my career, and helped the other night as Sam, Robert, and I discussed the players and filled our team. Before we started going through our individual yes and no kids, we set the following criteria to guide our decisions:

1. *Agree with goals* (**fun, learn, compete**)
2. *Parents' fit*
3. *Kids' fit*
4. *Talent appropriate*
5. *Capabilities complement one another*

1. *Agree with goals*

We started pouring through the questionnaires to see what light they shed on our situation. This data helped us determine who agreed with the goals: **fun, learn, compete**. I didn't rule anyone in from the questionnaire, but it did help me identify several kids and parents who likely would be happier with something different than we are creating. If there wasn't good alignment, better for everyone to know immediately and move in another direction. I believe the exercise made families think about these issues in a different way than they had before the tryout. This was a more insightful test than asking if everyone agreed with my philosophy. I was concerned that I'd just get a lot of head nodding and people telling me what they thought I wanted to hear.

2. *Parents' Fit*

I was only half joking when I told Sam and Robert that if I could only have one tryout, I would much prefer to have it for the parents, not the kids. Assembling a group of good people that have reasonable expectations for their kids and the coach is essential. Parents who yell at their kids, put enormous pressure on them, coach from the stands, or love the drama of continual conflict have no place on my team. I have more important things to occupy my time, and the controversy is never good for the kids. Unfortunately though, many parents can't separate their ego from what is ultimately best for their kid.

3. *Kids' Fit*

Most of the kids in youth sports are good kids. They all have at least a few rough edges, and that's part of our jobs as coaches to help sand them down a bit. But there are a few here and there that can make for some pretty bad team chemistry, like the kid who criticized others at the tryout while telling me he was the best player on the field.

4. *Talent Appropriate*

Determining if the kid's skill level was a good fit was the other non-baseball filter we used. It's important that players on the team have a similar amount of talent . . . ability grouping helps ensure they are not overmatched or bored by a lack of competition. It's not as big of a gap when the kids are young, but as they get to be nine or 10, the differences start to become an issue; at 11 and 12 they are profound. This is where coaches and parents have to make some tough decisions about where to place a kid. Even though Joey has played with a group of five other kids for the last three seasons, he's stopped growing and he doesn't have the skill to compete with them any longer.

This can make it tricky for a coach because parents are notorious for overrating the talent of their offspring. A friend who teaches high school orchestra says the same thing about the parents of budding violinists and cellists.

It's also difficult because some parents live vicariously through their son competing at the highest level possible. Their egos drive them to do anything to get their son on those teams, including even volunteering to coach if that will assure their kid a spot. Unfortunately, everyone knows what is going on, including the kid who is overmatched, failing, unhappy, frustrated, and has lost all self-confidence because he believes he's the weakest link on the team.

Within the last two weeks I've had two different coaches tell me they had parents say they were okay with their son being the 12th player on a team of 11 . . . they know he won't get much playing time but they want him to stay on the team and play at the higher level. I wonder who that is for . . . how is that helping the kid? Is that going to be fun? Is the parent fueling the kid's passion for the game? When he's 30 is he going to look back fondly with a nostalgic smile and proudly declare, "I warmed the bench . . . thanks, Dad"? Thankfully, both coaches said, "No thanks."

5. *Capabilities complement one another*

We didn't need eight first basemen on the team. We tried to arrange 11 players that complemented each other and give us the right amount of depth at each position.

We've ended up with kids who played on seven different teams last season. Alan and Nick need to have fun and the opportunity to play their positions. Anthony is coming up from recreational league and has a lot of fundamentals to learn. Dillon and Tyler lost all but one game last year and need to be in a more competitive environment. Brandon, Kaleb, Zach, and Tommy and are moving up from the instructional AA level and are looking for an additional challenge. Reed and Bobby are looking for a fresh start on a new team with more opportunity. It's a talented group with a lot of enthusiasm.

We'll have some team building to do, both with kids and parents, but I like the kids and I'm looking forward to getting to know them and their families better over the next eight or nine months.

Now I have to start making the phone calls to parents … 22 phone calls will take me all evening!

I made rookie mistake number one at the tryout the other day by giving the mouthy parent so much opportunity to talk before the event. I described the scene to a friend who is a seasoned coach. He laughed.

"Why did you let him do that?" he asked. "I would have cut him off and told him I wanted to see the kid perform without any preconceived ideas. I would have offered to talk to him after the tryout."

Good tip . . . had I not been so bogged down with equipment and logistics I might have thought of it myself . . . or maybe not. I suppose there are many things about coaching that only experience can teach you . . .

September 16

Making the Calls

Over the last 48 hours I've flashed back several times to the epic baseball movie, *Bull Durham*. Twice in the film, the manager of the Durham Bulls single-A pro team had to tell a player he was being released and that his services were no longer needed. He starts the conversation, "This is the toughest job a manager has . . . BUT, the organization has decided to make a change . . ."

It's no fun telling parents that it isn't going to work. It is part of the job, though, and I've been pounding the phone the last two evenings. I don't like being the guy who breaks the news that they need to keep searching for a team. I tried to be honest with parents, but at the same time give them hope and encouragement that they'll find the right situation. There were, however, a couple of exceptional cases that didn't come down to talent, numbers, or position alignment. These were the parental problems. Although I wanted to run fast and far from these people, I still had to be careful how I delivered that message.

It's unrealistic to expect a volunteer coach to tell a parent, "Yeah, I thought your kid has talent and he'd help us win a lot of games. You may be right; we might be a better team with him. However you and your husband are complete whack-jobs. Including you on my team would lead to conflict, anger, division, and eventually, outright rebellion of either the 10 sets of sane parents or the coaching staff or both. From the little I've witnessed, your presence would be a cancer that would eventually kill the spirit of this team. I'm not willing to endure nine months of that kind of torture. All of this means, unfortunately, your son will be penalized because your ego, dysfunctional personality, and/or misguided expectations of the kid, team, coach, and other parents is a hornet's nest I'm not willing to stir."

Yeah. Some things are better left unsaid.

I'm happy to report, though, I had only two sets of parents fit that mold. The worst of the two conversations started with mom. Upon hearing the news that I didn't have room for her son, she asked me no fewer than 15 questions about the other kids on my team, what their qualifications were, why I had selected them, and why they were better choices than her son. Of course I didn't provide answers, but it certainly didn't stop her from asking. Woodward and Bernstein were less thorough while interrogating sources as they broke Watergate. But I held the line.

Her suggestion was that, since she wasn't satisfied with my explanation, I call her husband on his cell phone. Although he was on business travel, she assured me he would have questions she wasn't able to think of on such short notice. She actually gave me the number believing I'd call.

I have to admit, as painful as that conversation was, it pales with the story told by a coaching buddy. After his tryout, two sets of parents became irate as he made his personnel decisions on the spot. Initially they questioned him in similar fashion to what I went through. But then it turned ugly. They demanded to see his evaluation forms. This vigilante group wanted proof that the other kids rated higher than theirs. The coach slinked away to shouts, insults, and threats of lawsuit.

Most of my conversations though, were short and to the point. My explanations were about skill levels and numbers. And those parents, while disappointed, understood the situation and accepted the news, ready to move on. I genuinely wished them well.

I'm glad it's over. The biggest eye-opener in this whole tryout/selection/notification process has been how terrible parents are at assessing the talent of their kids. They can do a pretty good job of determining skill levels of players if their son is not on the field; put him in the mix, though, and the parent becomes incapable of objectively ranking the kids' abilities. They lose perspective, they rationalize, and they include their hopes, dreams, and the voices of their egos in the assessment. I'm now a believer that tryouts are helpful, if not essential. It's critical that coaches help determine the level at which kids should compete.

Now I'm ready to begin the baseball part of being a baseball coach. We have 11 kids and their parents ready to make a journey together. Opening day can't get here fast enough!

Part II

Spring Training

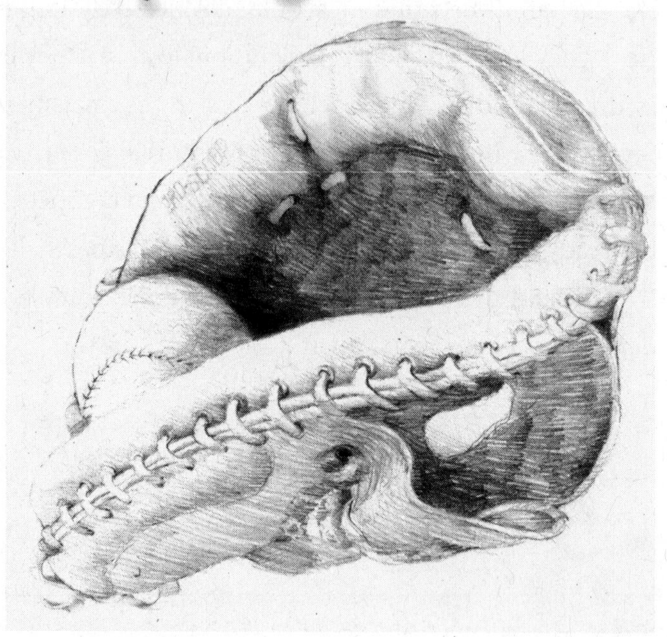

January 12

Multiple Sport Athletes

There's snow on the ground and the days are short, but the team has done good work in the batting cages. Our approach is to break the 11 kids into small groups for batting practice once or twice a week. With only four or five players per session we are more productive and I get to know each kid better and provide more individualized instruction. This schedule, though, means I'm busy three or four nights a week. Several kids juggle this with practice and game schedules of their other sports. Four kids play basketball on three different teams (each with its own schedule) and one is wrestling.

The overlap between the seasons of youth sports is only getting worse as the kids get older, and it is, I believe, a troubling trend in youth sports. Many coaches in all sports frown on their athletes playing other sports because it interferes with their efforts throughout the year. They pressure (or coerce) kids to choose one sport at an early age. The logic, stated or implied, is that if some of their teammates play year-round, then to remain competitive or risk losing their spot, they must specialize. That's a shame. The coaches win and the kids lose.

I have two rules of thumb:

1. *Kids should play as many sports as they want to for as long as they can.*

2. *The sport in season should get priority.*

Take basketball for example. There are leagues year-round because court time is always available (except, ironically, in-season). Many coaches expect their kids to play all the time. The theory is that if kids are constantly on the court, then when the season rolls around they'll be better than the kids that played football, baseball, or lacrosse. However, it's the program — not the individual kids — that enjoys the biggest gains. Developing teamwork, choreographing defenses, and memorizing plays takes time and practice. Drilling this for 12 months is great for the program. But is it healthy for the kids? Probably not.

Burnout is the obvious first reason. Playing the same sport every day for long periods of time — no matter how much you love it — is a recipe for mental fatigue. I did a quick search on the Internet for "youth sports burnout" and dozens of articles popped up. Again and again they describe kids dropping out of sports all together as they hit their teenage years because, among other reasons related to coach and parental pressure, it just wasn't fun anymore.

Sports have become like work for these single sport kids. They slog to practices showing the same sense of drudgery that many adults display for their eight-to-five jobs. The articles described 10-year-olds practicing soccer four days a week and then playing multiple games on weekends in year-round leagues. Players faked injuries so they wouldn't have to play anymore. Even worse, several kids expressed relief when doctors diagnosed season- or career-ending injuries.

These greedy coaches willingly sacrifice several players in their General Patton-like march towards league championships. With trophy in hand, they all-too-easily replace the casualties with a new batch of recruits eager to play in a great winning program. Who are the real winners? Shouldn't kids get the most benefit from youth sports?

Finally, many articles warn of the dangers of using growing bones and muscles in the same way year-round. Forget the mental monotony for a moment, the repetitive motion of same game, same skills and same drills is often a recipe for stress fractures, growth-plate disruption, and a wide variety of over-use injuries.

It's important to recall that kids take the field because they love the game, enjoy playing with their friends, and relish the thrill of competition. These are the driving forces for youth athletes, not winning or preparing for high school, college, and professional ball. Too many kids get robbed of their childhood fun by the coach's ego . . . and his misguided aspirations of one day coaching the high school team.

Perhaps the most important reason kids should not specialize is that each sport they play gives them new and different insights into themselves as competitors that may be difficult to learn any other way. The quickness and aggressiveness Jimmy learned in football last fall makes him a better base runner this spring. The patience Joey learns waiting for a good pitch to hit makes him a better passing guard in basketball. The different equipment, skills, rules, and approaches to the game that make each sport uniquely fun also make kids better all-round athletes. That was my experience in high school.

Playing basketball taught me several things that made me a better baseball player. They are lessons I probably wouldn't have learned as quickly or completely playing just baseball. I enjoyed basketball through my junior year in high school, but I clearly wasn't going to play in college. I wasn't a ball handler or a pure shooter and I wasn't big enough to bang inside with the really big guys. But I enjoyed playing. And I was able to contribute to the team's success by getting loads of rebounds, playing defense, and diving for every loose ball on the floor.

I remember one game I was giving up about four inches in height and at least 40 pounds to the big man inside. For some reason, I ended up guarding this gorilla and I got pummeled. I kept trying to play my typical game, which worked against smaller guys, but this goon was pushing me all over the place. It seemed like he scored every time down the court and if I dared take a shot, he blocked it … spectacularly.

By the second quarter I was beat up. During a timeout I started venting some frustration to a teammate in the huddle. Coach Garrison paused, glared at me, and told me to stop whining. He said I needed to find a way to beat the guy. The only other choice was for me to give up. He asked me very pointedly if I wanted to do that. I fumbled for words, surprised that he didn't take my side and sympathize that I had a tough assignment. Finally I admitted that I didn't want to quit. He stared at me in silence for a few moments and then suggested a few different things to try.

I was mad. I was frustrated by the goon who had been brutalizing my body and ego, and still a little angry with my coach. I hustled back on the floor and the next time they brought the ball down the court I tried a few of his ideas. I changed my defensive approach to deny the pass, and on offense looked first to set a pick for my teammates. It worked! I didn't shut the guy down completely. He still had a great game. Eventually I think I fouled out near the end of the third quarter, but this mostly frustrating experience taught me how critical tenacity is when things aren't going well. I learned that to be successful, you have to adjust during the game. I know those things made me a better pitcher the next season.

Later that year I learned another important lesson playing a pick-up game. The guy guarding me was really good — not so much in his quickness or shooting, but he was so fundamentally sound it took me completely out of my game. He always boxed out on shots (put his body between me and the basket so I couldn't rebound), denied passes to me underneath, and out-hustled me in just about every situation (not quickness, hustle). I found out later that he played college basketball. His effort showed me how completely frustrating it is to play against someone who executes the fundamentals correctly on every play.

Afterwards I thought about how executing the fundamentals applied to baseball. I saw that it didn't matter if it was pickoffs to keep base runners close, backing up home plate, or covering first on a ball hit to the right side of the infield, doing things the right way every time would make me better. The experience on the court showed me that my discipline would weigh on my opponents. Just like the guy boxing me out on every shot, I wasn't going to give my adversaries anything they didn't earn. The college player forced me to play his style of basketball, which put tremendous pressure on me because I felt I had to take advantage of every opportunity. I began to think about how I could do that on the mound.

I'm not sure I would have learned either of those lessons quite that quickly or that thoroughly on the baseball diamond. If I had played only baseball I might not have had as much success without incorporating those nuggets into my game. I'm glad my coaches and parents didn't pressure me into focusing on just one sport.

Alan had a similar experience with football last fall. There was pressure to play baseball in the fall because several teammates had registered for the league. Alan thought about playing so he'd get better at throwing a change up — a pitch that could set him apart as a 12-year-old. But he also really wanted to give football a try. Although I was concerned about injury, I'm glad he did. He had a blast. He applied lessons learned about hard work in baseball to the football field. And he's starting to translate the athletic aggressiveness required for defensive end to his approach on the mound and in the batters box.

The point is that having success in a sport — any sport — unlocks barriers to performance that can be translated to any sport or endeavor. Often these are mental obstacles of connecting hard work to performance or overcoming the big barrier of "I can't." Confidence as an athlete transcends the sport, especially at the younger ages. Learning, as a defensive end, to believe you can get around the big mean offensive tackle, and then adjusting your approach and finding a way to do it, trains the mind and body to believe. Then the next time you're standing in the batters box against the big mean lefty on the mound, it is much easier to believe you can get a hit. You use those same mental muscles to adjust and find a way to put the bat on the ball. It's the same challenge . . . only the skills and circumstances are different.

Ultimately, we have to remember why we are here. It's to help the kids *learn, compete, develop,* and *enjoy* playing sports. As coaches of youth our greatest aspirations should be that they have no regrets when they are our age . . . the worst scenario is the adult that picks up his son's ball glove, smells the leather, pounds the pocket with his fist, and laments, "I wish I would have played baseball another season or two when I was 11."

My other rule of thumb is that kids need to give the sport in season their full attention. For those in basketball or wrestling, I'm asking one hour one night a week and I am juggling my availability to accommodate their schedules. If there's a conflict, I tell them to play the sport in season and I'll work with them another night or the following week.

I'll expect the same respect this spring and summer . . . and I know I won't always get it from other coaches.

Coaches set the expectations and build the schedules, but it is the kids and parents who ultimately make the decisions on how and where they'll spend their time and focus their efforts. During Alan's football season one of the kids on the team decided to play in an early-fall basketball league. The hoops coach mandated a practice on the same night as we already had football practice. The parents and kid wanted to miss football one night a week so he could play both sports.

Alan's football coach rightfully pointed out to the parents that this wasn't fair to the football team. Back in August the kid made a commitment to the football team. If he wasn't at practice the kid wouldn't know the plays nor would he be improving as much or as quickly as his teammates. All of this would hurt the football team. Alan's coach said that it would be okay if he could practice basketball another night so that it wouldn't interfere, but it wasn't fair to the football team to give half effort and attention. Even though it was an off-season basketball league, the parents decided to have him play both and he missed half the practices of both sports.

Unfortunately I believe many coaches wring everything they can from the kid and family. But what does that teach the kids? It's okay to over-commit and do things half way? Shouldn't we be teaching them to do a few things very well, rather than setting unrealistic expectations that they can and should do everything all the time? What are we role-modeling for our kids? Shouldn't we emphasize quality of experience over quantity of activity? Half-assed efforts waste everyone's time. It comes back to a central question . . . is the goal to help the kids enjoy youth sports or to build a coaching dynasty?

January 16

Fun and Learning at Practice

I've been thinking about the research I've read about burnout, playing multiple sports, and keeping things fun for kids. While there's some tweaking I'll do to our indoor batting cage practice sessions, I think the approach is sound. I realize that several of the kids are practicing other sports twice during the week, so my hitting sessions need to be short, instructional, and fun.

We're taking a quick round of batting practice, starting with soft toss or hitting off the tee and progress to live pitching. We videotape the last several swings for each of the four or five kids. We then go on the other room and watch them on the big television. They love it.

Dissecting the swings is great instruction and the kids learn a lot seeing themselves in the act of swinging a bat. They are often surprised at what they do versus what they think they do. The camera doesn't lie.

Something I didn't plan on was the comedy routine they enact with the video camera running. The batter is usually the only serious one as his teammates are hamming it up with commentary. They are having fun with this mostly unstructured playtime together, something the research said was important for kids of all ages.

After we laugh and learn from the video, we go back in the cage for another round or two of live pitching. We then have some sort of hitting or bunting contest, which is when the comedy commentary turns to trash talking and bravado. In just a few weeks I've already seen improvement in every one of the kids. And they're having so much fun they don't want to leave. I didn't design it this way on purpose. It just evolved. It's a good recipe . . . instruction, learning, loose structure, fun, and play. My challenge will be to continue this formula when we get outside with larger groups.

February 17

Responding by Focusing on the Positive

I was disappointed in our practice indoors last night. The kids weren't focused, they lacked energy and enthusiasm and a few were goofing off at different times. It's tough to play baseball in an elementary school gymnasium, but with snow blanketing the ground, it's what we have to work with.

At the end of practice I huddled the kids and told them I was disappointed in their level of effort. That needed to be said to reinforce my expectations and improve their performance in the future. I didn't, however, want to leave the conversation on that sour note. I thought about **fun, learn, compete**.

"Look, guys," I explained, "to be competitive, we have to get more benefit out of our practices, even if we are inside. There was too much horsing around and not enough effort in the drills and getting better. I know you guys know how to do this, and in fact I saw flashes of it here tonight."

I then singled out each kid, praising him for at least one positive thing I saw him do. Whether it was hitting wiffle balls, using good throwing technique, supporting a teammate, or hustling in between drills, I gave each kid a positive takeaway.

In addition to giving them encouragement, this served one other purpose: I wanted them to know I was paying attention to what they were doing. I wanted to subtly remind them that although I can't see everything that happens, coaches are more aware than the kids might think. As I recounted the good behaviors, the energy of the team changed. There were more smiles and they were much more tuned in to what I was saying.

Then I ended things with a reminder for positive action. "These are the things we have to do if we're going to be competitive and have more fun this season. Let's have a better practice this weekend, huh?" I got a lot of "yeah, coach" and then they put their hands in the middle and said a "Yellow Jackets on three" cheer to break the huddle.

In terms of *Respond* and *React*, I could have torn into the group for poor effort. Overlooking the fact that I built the practice plan and need to take ownership for not getting the results, it would have felt good to vent my frustration a bit. But that would have been a downer for the kids, especially this early in the season. There's no need to use a sledgehammer when a tap on the shoulder might do the trick.

Instead, I think they understood my expectations for effort at practice. I accept the fact that over the course of a long season we'll have some lackluster efforts in both practice and games. In this case I believe I *Responded* by looking at the larger picture — I focused them on the things I want more of. As a result, I hope I fueled their desire to get better and work hard. If I don't see a difference over the weekend, I can escalate the intensity of my *Response* and there will probably be several kids running sprints or doing pushups if they can't focus and give the necessary effort.

February 25

Mortgaging for Metal and the Joy of Wood

The phenomenon of sticker shock has expanded beyond the big hunks of metal with four wheels to the slender rods of alloy that kids use to hit a baseball. I was shopping at the local batting cage facility yesterday, hoping to pick up a decent metal bat for Alan's birthday. I browsed through the merchandise area, all the while hearing the hollow, high-pitched "tings" and "tinks" from the 12 batting tubes in this strip mall turned athletic facility.

The first bat I picked up was a sleek red and white one with a -8.5 proudly plastered across the barrel indicating the difference between the weight and length. I twisted the barrel slightly to read the price . . . $219. I quickly returned the bat to the rack, hoping I hadn't scratched or otherwise damaged it, which might make me in some way responsible to buy the thing. Not having shopped for higher performance bats, I reasoned that I had probably selected the most expensive one first . . . dream on! A brutish gold and navy bat next caught my eye. It was a top-of-the-line -3 model for high school use. $399. Plus tax. Some quick math put this puppy at nearly $200 per pound. I assumed it came with either a payment plan or an application for a second mortgage.

To gather my wits, get some perspective, and think twice about making a purchase, I slinked out of the gift shop area and watched some of the high school players take batting practice. I was awestruck by the power and velocity of their swings and how fast the ball jumped off their bats. There was one kid, a high school senior I later discovered, using one of those navy and gold beauties. He was, in a word, a monster. His swing was compact and fine-tuned, but it also had a frightening wild animal strength and speed that actually scared me a bit. And I was on the other side of two nets. His primal grunts and the length of his follow through added to the presence he brought to the plate. I saw him crush every pitch, the ball sizzling through the tube and hitting the back of the net or tagging the pitching screen and pushing it back a few inches. I decided that there was no way I would throw batting practice to this guy. Simply put, it didn't look safe.

I meandered back to the gift shop, my world thoroughly rocked first by the price tags of the merchandise and then the brute force with which these metal bats were swung these days. Trying to find some familiar ground, I asked the high school kid behind the register if anyone besides adults used wood bats anymore. He looked at me with amused yet sympathetic eyes, as if I had asked whether hula skirts and penny loafers were still in style.

"Nope, not really," he said, shaking his head. His facial expression screamed "Dude, you are totally old school" as he looked me over head to toe.

I chewed on that for a moment and pondered the economics.

"Well, I suppose if you spend $400 for a bat, you'll get several seasons out of it," I reasoned, trying to make the leap in my mind. Perhaps I just needed to look at it as an investment . . . and, let's see, amortized over several years . . . uh . . . yep, still darned expensive.

The kid did a great job resisting the urge to roll his eyes but couldn't hold back the "got a novice over here, boss" look. "Not really," he explained. "The metal will fatigue after a while, especially if you're taking BP everyday. I went through three of those last year."

Although my cerebral cortex was momentarily stunned, my reptilian brain could still do the math. "You spent $1,200 on bats last season?" I blurted without thinking.

"Uh, yeeeah," he said with a cavalier tone, indicating mom and dad footed the bill. I nodded and wandered back to the rack, trying to look interested without showing shock and awe on my face. I'm sure it was his 15 minutes of customer service training that stopped him from saying, "Thanks for coming in, old guy," as I ambled away.

The economics, however, only tell part of the story behind the debate between wood and metal bats. There are two other facets to the issue: safety and purity of the game.

In terms of safety, a number of industry studies seem to show that injuries are no more likely to happen with metal bats than they are with their wood counterparts. To be certified by The Little League®, metal bats have to meet criteria that ensure the bat does not create ball speeds greater than those achieved by the best wood bats. But I still read reports of terrible injuries to kids who had no chance to react to a ball being smashed in their direction.

I'm not sure what to believe. I'd like to hope that everyone involved has youth safety, and not the almighty dollar, motivating their actions. I will argue though, that there will be more balls hit hard with metal bats than with wood bats. The "sweet spot" for a wood bat — the largest portion of the barrel that will produce the most solid hit — is only a few inches long. To make the bat balanced and light enough for a mere mortal to swing, the barrel has to quickly taper down in diameter. So any ball hitting this tapered part will not have the maximum force behind it.

With a metal bat, however, the sweet spot could be eight or even 10 inches in length. So a hitter with a metal bat can be sloppy, slow, fooled, awkward, out of position, lazy, or just an average talent and still get the sweet spot on the ball and hit it with authority. Eye-popping batting averages in high schools and colleges confirm that more balls are hit harder with metal bats. Hitting .400 with a metal bat seems to be blasé these days. When you look at batting averages in professional ball, though, with wood bats the required equipment, .300 is still the gold standard.

And, my personal, and admittedly biased, experience tells me that metal bats produce harder hit balls. I've hit with both during the same BP session and the metal bats make the ball jump faster and further than the wood bats do. I can feel it and I can see it. And from the other side of the plate, when I throw BP I notice an immediate difference when the batter drops the wood bat and picks up the metal . . . night and day. Yep, human emotions, biased perception, a small sample size, and no hard data to quantify the velocity and forces involved. I fully admit all of those fallacies exist in my reasoning. But you'll never convince me that metal bats are equally or less dangerous than wood.

So with my bias out in the open, I'll conclude my rant with a short discussion about purity of the game. Everyone knows that the cheap "tink" of a metal bat is a flimsy replacement for the wholesome "crack" of a wood bat. While these aesthetics are important, baseball though, above all, is a game of merit. Everyone gets a lucky hit once in a while . . . the little blooper that falls in just beyond a fielder's reach. But then a diving shortstop robs us of a single to left and all is even.

All baseball players know they must earn what they get. Metal bats, though, reward mediocrity. Average hitters shouldn't hit .400. They should hit .250. Giving them a 10-inch sweet spot to hit the ball demeans the effort of a pitcher. Putting this type of technology in the hands of an average hitter enables him to get a base hit 40 percent of the time . . . this is no different than giving every kid a trophy for mere participation. Success and accomplishment must be earned, not given away or purchased for $399.

So here's my beef. The guy on the mound works hard to set up a hitter for a certain pitch. He's busted two fastballs in on the hitter's hands and gotten two quick strikes with foul balls. The batter now has timed his swing to the pitcher's hard stuff and is ready for another heater. The pitcher hurls the expected high fastball with a little extra velocity to pop the catcher's glove and reinforce to the hitter that he does, in fact, throw hard. The hitter, earning a bit of credit here, doesn't fall for the high cheese, and takes the pitch for ball one. Now, with the count one ball and two strikes, the pitcher has set his trap and moves in for the kill.

The pitcher pauses on the mound to savor the moment, staring in at the catcher for an extra beat or two. He then winds up and throws a beautiful changeup low and away. It starts on the very outside corner of the plate just above the knees and, over the course of 40 or 45 feet, floats ever so gently a little further outside and drops four or five inches so that it is now fully below the batter's knee cap.

The hitter is completely fooled. At this point, it still looks just like a fastball. And, having been busted inside with a couple of pitches, he's not mentally prepared to reach out over the plate. So the pitcher has immediately earned an advantage by setting up this wicked pitch. He's trained the batter to look for something that won't be there. The hitter has seen three fastballs zip through the zone, and, with two strikes, he's determined that another one will not sneak by him.

So he swings early and swings hard.

While the location of this pitch certainly helps, it is the speed of the changeup that ultimately slays the hitter; his swing is calibrated to the pace of those three nasty fastballs. As the hitter's over-anxious bat swings through the zone, the lazy changeup still has five more feet to travel before it reaches the plate.

Oops . . . he's swung too fast and too soon . . . and the ball is on the far side of the plate, even further from his reach. Instead of a short, powerful compact swing he's perfected in the batting cage, the hitter's arms are outstretched awkwardly, his head and neck jerked around, his butt is pushed out in an effort to reach this pitch, and he's completely off balance. It's a thing of beauty. The hitter looks awkward, is fooled, out of position and, at least in this at-bat, overmatched. The pitcher outsmarted and overpowered him.

With the ball still five feet from the plate, the batter realizes his predicament and has learned to keep his hands back just long enough to slow the bat down. This allows the barrel to hang around and wait for the ball. Even though the batter's body is out of position and the bat speed is now half or a third of a normal swing, he just barely makes contact with the last two inches of the barrel.

In this scenario, a wooden bat will, at best, produce a slow roller to the second baseman. At worst the bat will shatter and the pitcher will dodge flying chunks of wood, calmly walk over and collect the ball, and gently toss it to the first baseman for the out. Either way, the pitcher relishes his victory.

But our hitter has bought himself out of the jam with his shiny alloy stick. The $399 purchase means the last two inches of the barrel is still the sweet spot. Even though his swing is slow and clunky this ball will be hit just hard enough to arc over the second baseman's head and land softly in the outfield grass. The batter jogs down to first base shaking his head, knowing he got fooled but thinking he deserved a hit anyway. "Good piece of hitting there. Way to adjust," he mutters, giving himself a pat on the back.

The pitcher is shaking his head even more vigorously, the voice inside saying, "You've got to be kidding me. That was a nasty pitch! What do I have to do to get somebody out? What sort of karma am I working through to be that unlucky?"

The concept of justice is merely a pipe dream in a world with metal bats. The hitter shouldn't be standing on first base, enjoying a slightly higher batting average for his effort. Instead, he should be sitting at the end of the bench, slowly removing his batting gloves, replaying the at-bat in his mind, realizing that the pitcher got him out and didn't even throw one pitch that the umpire would have called a strike.

I know, I know . . . I'm talking like a pitcher, so I'll end my rant by affirming that there is no sweeter sound in the game of baseball than the splintering of an ash bat and the immediate growl of the batter (a heartfelt expletive is even better) as he stumbles out of the batter's box pondering which is more painful: the vibrating buzz in his hands, the anguish of being responsible for the ball feebly rolling towards an infielder for an easy out, or the sting to his wallet for $40 to replace his lumber.

Baseball should reward effort and skill, not technology and purchasing power.

March 7

The Seeding Tournament

This weekend we play in the league's annual seeding tournament. It's a series of games that determine which level the 24 teams at the 12-year-old division will play. Eight teams will be majors, 10 will be AAA, and six will be AA. It comes down to two games. To qualify for AAA we have to win one of two. If we lose both, we end up AA, and winning both gets us a majors berth.

It's pretty nerve-wracking. I believe we are a AAA-caliber team, but since we haven't played any games and, thanks to the weather, we've have had only one scrimmage, I really don't know how good — or bad — we are.

I feel tremendous pressure to get this right. End up at AA and we'll probably mop the floor with those teams; finish in majors and we'll likely get pounded all season. The success of the entire season depends to a large degree on the games we play this weekend — they determine how competitive we'll be, have huge bearing on how much fun we have, and the impact amount our kids will learn. Those are the three keys to success we defined last fall . . . seems a bit unfair that so much of it rides on the first two games of the season.

March 12

Our Defining Moment — Defeating the Rustlers

We qualified for the AAA level! Last night was an amazing way to start the season. We beat the Rustlers with an unbelievable pitching performance and last-inning rally. It had all the pressure of a late-season playoff game and the drama of a seesaw battle between two evenly matched teams. And to top it off, Alan got the clutch hit to drive in the tying run and then scored the go-ahead run in the top of the last inning. The victory assures that we'll play the AAA level, but more importantly it was exactly the experience we needed to gel as a team. We are no longer a collection of recreational league, AA, and AAA players from seven different teams who happen to be playing together. We are now the Yellow Jackets, 11 kids who are becoming fast friends on a bona fide AAA team.

I think I felt more pressure than the kids; the combined weight of our expectations seemed to fall squarely on my shoulders. The coaches, players, and parents all felt AAA would be the best competitive challenge, so this game against the Rustlers was a big one.

It was close the whole way, tied 3 - 3 entering the fourth inning. They held us scoreless in the top half even though we had two hits. In the bottom half of the fourth they got a one-out hit, stole second, and then after a strikeout, had a bloop single to left that scored the go-ahead run.

We went quickly and silently in the top of the fifth . . . two groundouts and a popup to the pitcher. Of more concern to me, however, was the time limit — the umpire said we had eight minutes remaining from the 1:45 allotted for the game. No new inning could begin after time expired, which meant we had to get three outs in the bottom of the fifth in less than eight minutes.

Bobby, our pitcher, sprinted out to the mound and told the umpire he didn't need any warm up throws. The umpire bellowed, "Batter up!" and Bobby went to work. It was one of the most impressive pitching performances I've seen in youth sports. Not only did he have to work fast, but he had to throw strikes. He did both . . . all amid the baseball drama unfolding and under the enormous pressure of needing to win because of what this game could mean to the success of our season.

He struck out the first batter on four pitches and got the next batter to ground out to second base.

Two outs.

Clock ticking.

The next batter took a strike and then lined a solid single to centerfield.

Tick, tick, tick, tick.

I grimaced. That was going to break our back.

I was sure time was about to expire.

Bobby got the ball and quickly threw another strike. The batter popped it up to Alan at third base. As the ball landed in his glove to record the third out, the next inning technically would start . . . as long as we had not reached the time limit.

I immediately turned towards the home plate umpire. He was already looking at his watch, calculating the time limit based on the game's start time.

He looked up and announced to the field, "One minute left. This will be the last inning." Our bench and section of the bleachers erupted in a huge cheer! I breathed a sigh of relief. I knew that if we had another opportunity to bat we'd come back and score. We had the heart of our lineup coming to the plate. I liked our chances.

I turned to our dugout to give them a motivational talk and immediately realized it wouldn't be necessary. Everyone had mobbed Bobby as they left the field, practically carrying him into the dugout. I was now hearing comments like, "This game is ours," "Let's go get them!" and "All we need is two runs!"

Yep, they were motivated. We still, though, needed a bit of instruction and focus. "Look guys, we don't have to hurry anymore," I explained. "Time isn't a factor. Be patient hitters up there. Make their pitcher throw strikes and hit the ball hard somewhere. We don't need homeruns, we need base runners."

Fittingly, Bobby led of the inning with another chance to be a hero. He walked on five pitches, bringing Alan to the plate. I had Bobby steal second base on the first pitch, which placed the tying run in scoring position with nobody out. Alan already had driven in two of our three runs with two solid hits. He took a ball and then fouled off two pitches.

Alan laced the next pitch over the shortstop's head into left centerfield, splitting the two outfielders. Bobby scored easily and Alan trotted into second with a double. As our dugout erupted with noise, Alan raised both arms over his head, I suppose in excitement, pride, and triumph. Whatever it was I had a lump in my throat and felt tears welling up.

The next pitch got away from the catcher, advancing Alan to third. Nick singled to centerfield and Alan crossed the plate to make it 5 - 4. We got two more runs and I felt comfortable entering the bottom of the sixth up by three. Bobby finished the game strong, giving up only one hit. The final play was a ground ball to Brandon at shortstop and we all celebrated the final out near first base after Reed caught the throw and had his foot touching the bag.

I was relieved. What a stressful two hours! I'm glad we won, but the way we won and how the team came together at the end was more than I could have hoped for. Not bad for game one! In the restaurant after the game the kids celebrated like they were friends, laughing, joking and teasing each other. Teambuilding experts would be amazed at how quickly we have bonded. We're now officially a AAA team . . . I'm now looking forward to opening day.

March 15

Keeping Score

A couple of weeks ago, Billy, one of the parents, asked me if I had a scorekeeper. When I replied, "No, not yet, but I am looking for a qualified volunteer," his eyes lit up and he said he'd be happy to take on the responsibility. This was the beginning of what I hope will be a symbiotic relationship between scorekeeper and coach. Since then we've had several conversations about the importance of keeping score and how we could use the data collected in the book.

Keeping score is a required task for the home team because their book is the official score. The umpire arbitrates any disputes between the teams after examining the home team's book. The visitors keep their version, and ideally, the two scorekeepers confer after each half inning to make sure they are in agreement, as if balancing a checkbook.

The value of the scorebook, though, goes far beyond counting to see who has the most runs at the end of the game. The intricate notations, symbols, and numerology a scorekeeper uses to catalogue every play also open an expansive dimension to the game of baseball: statistics that can be compared across players, teams, and time.

While watching a game from the seventh row, the game of baseball provides a competitive drama that appeals to our right brain, which appreciates feelings and flow, looking at the whole picture before examining its parts. The athletes' performance, no matter if they are seven-year-old rec-league players or recognizable names in a late season Yankees-Red Sox matchup, is a thing of beauty, on par with other creative endeavors like dance, theater, or ballet.

Baseball though, also appeals to the left brain, and that's where the logic and structure of the scorekeeping system create an analytic undercurrent that separates it from other sports and activities. The mathematical symmetry of three strikes, three outs, three sets of three innings, nine player positions, etc. is captured in a grid of small diamonds and squares to keep track of balls, strikes, hits, walks, errors, and runs. This wealth of information, with its organization and complexity, permits a complete recreation of the game, hours, days, or even centuries later, and precipitates statistics that not only allow, but also encourage comparisons between teammates or even players separated by 80 years of history.

These numbers and symbols, though, can't adequately describe the beauty of a diving backhand catch by the third baseman and his phenomenal throw from his knees to get the batter by a half a step at first. It is simply scored 5 – 3. Nor can the system tell you the flaw in a pitcher's mechanics that leads to six walks in four innings. So watching the game with an eye to appreciating the beauty of the performance ***and*** reading the scorebook are two sides of the same coin. The elegance of the event delights our right brain while the analytical left brain adores the piles of data a single nine-inning game produces.

I use the book to help me understand the game in a way that isn't visible to the naked eye. Simply, my mind isn't capable of keeping all of that data straight as the action happens, because there are scores of other things I'm trying to remember to say or do in the heat of the moment.

The statistics help paint a more complete picture of a player's performance and contribution to the team, enabling me to better identify and fix problems. For example, I may notice that Jimmy hasn't gotten a hit in his last eight times to the plate. As I look through the scorebook, I see that most of the time he has two strikes on him when he finally puts the ball in play. I'm now aware of a tendency. As I think back to his last few times at the plate, I realize he's watching the first few pitches go by — he's not swinging the bat. With this knowledge I can have a discussion with Jimmy about being more aggressive. I can ask the right questions to understand why he's watching strikes go by . . . is he afraid of swinging and missing . . . is he not seeing the ball well . . . is he just not pulling the trigger? Now I can provide instruction and drills to help him break the slump. I might not have seen any of this without the cold hard data the scorebook provides.

The same is true for the team as a whole. If we lose a close game we might all focus on the two errors we made in the last inning. I'll deduce that more work is needed on fielding ground balls and making accurate throws to first base. That's probably warranted. However, while reviewing the scorebook in my easy chair with a cup of coffee the next morning, I discover that we left 12 runners on base in the six innings and we had only two hits in 17 at-bats with runners in scoring position. Now my next practice will include discussion about the importance of driving in runs and working on the mental part of hitting in clutch situations. I'll develop a drill to reward kids for putting the ball in play to score runs. This data also tells me I may need to adjust my coaching strategy to scratch and claw for more runs with bunts, steals, or hit-and-run plays. I might need to be more aggressive, taking chances to get the extra base.

Billy and I talked, though, about being careful with the statistics we gather. Sharing them with young players can often do more damage than good because kids often don't understand what the numbers mean . . . they simply compare themselves to one another. This can bring out the worst in kids . . . and adults! While the statistics may be helpful for coaches, I don't think they are meaningful to kids younger than nine or 10. Some might argue they should be even older before giving them a hearty dose of numbers. The other danger is that some kids, no matter the age, will focus too much on their own individual numbers, preferring to get two hits in three at-bats rather than enjoy a team win.

My plan is to share the data with the coaches every week or so and talk about the trends we see and make necessary adjustments. I'll show the kids their individual statistics a couple of times throughout the year, but they'll only see their numbers and the team totals. When I do share them with the kids, I'll take the time to explain what the numbers mean and what each player needs to do to improve.

I think Billy will be an extremely valuable asset to the team and me this year. His experience and knowledge of the game will give me insight of tremendous value, and he'll be able to provide perspective I won't be able to get any other way.

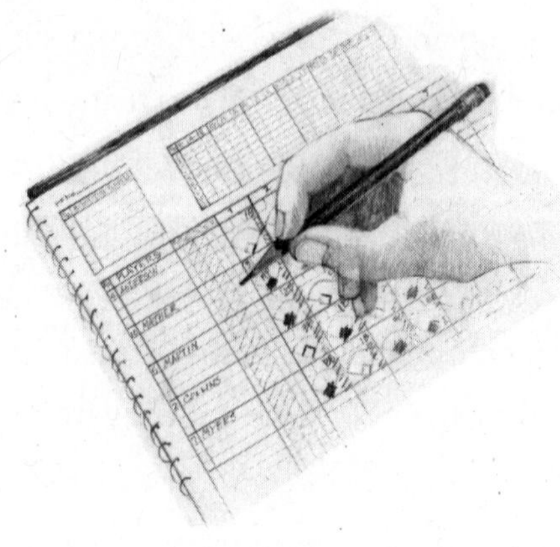

March 20

Bullpen Catcher

I've always thought that one of the best jobs in the world would be major league bullpen catcher. I'd travel with all of the big leaguers, have great seats to all the games, get to walk through the clubhouse, and hang out with the players. In return I'd sit and eat sunflower seeds for six innings and then grab my glove and catch the pitchers warming up in the bullpen. Okay, so there's specialized knowledge required to help the pitchers with their release points and other mechanics while providing feedback on the movement of their different pitches that night. Fine. I love a professional challenge.

However, last night I realize I've taken for granted the catching part. The last time I caught was one inning in a blowout game after 9th grade . . . my approach quickly became, wait until the ball stops rolling turn around and go pick it up. But those pitchers in the major league pen are throwing exploding fastballs popping the glove with 90+ m.p.h. force, wicked sliders darting across the plate, breaking balls that fall off the proverbial table, and cut fastballs that will collapse your chest if you blink and don't move your glove at the last second. But hey, I played baseball in college. I'm an athlete. Bring it on.

Last night I was catching a few of our pitchers and set up in the outfield with my back to the fence so, in case I missed one, I wouldn't have far to run. It was cold, the grass was wet, and a gentle breeze quickly numbed exposed skin. On about the fourth pitch, Nick uncorked a fastball that, simply, I couldn't handle. The pitching distance was 50 feet, but the ball traveled about 47.5. I couldn't decide which way to turn my glove. Flip and scoop or turn and reach? Now I know what I should have done, but in that small fraction of a second I had to decide, I got caught halfway.

Although my "studly," college athlete mind and ego believed I had the play made, my 42-year-old body knew otherwise. Give it some credit. Admittedly I've lost speed, but I've learned to compensate with anticipation. Not enough though. It's too depressing to calculate accurately, but the net loss in ability is I'm sure more than 50 percent. As the ball approached the ground, my legs quickly swung to my right, revealing to the world that I must not be wearing a cup. My head jerked wildly up and to the left, ensuring I would never see the ball as it struck me. My glove was pocket facing down, about four inches above the ball, as it skipped off the damp grass.

I felt a quick, sharp sting as the Rawlings leather impacted my ankle. A direct hit on a damp 35-degree evening. Even though I had on sweat pants the laces left two small purplish-red bruise marks. The pain was severe but it paled to the agony my inner 18-year-old athlete endured watching a 42-year-old botch this catch. Oh, the shame.

However, I did hop up fast, bouncing rapidly on my one good leg, vigorously shaking the damaged one in the air. At that moment I noticed a jogging trail just behind the outfield fence. A fit, athletic-looking runner cruised by — the only one I'd seen in 45 minutes on this cold night.

He witnessed the whole thing, and, without breaking stride, said, "Nice form, coach," and vanished into the night.

I won't be applying for the bullpen catcher job anytime soon.

The Role of a Coach

Coaches have to see themselves as leaders of their teams, not just managers of a long list of tasks. A leader and a manager are two different roles. Leaders establish a vision, set direction, and create the tone or culture of the team. They help players and parents better understand the context of on- and off-the-field events and how those align, or don't, with the goals and direction of the team. They keep the team on course towards success.

A manager executes a vision by handling the hundreds of tasks and decisions required to achieve success. A good manager pokes, prods, pushes and pulls the team in that already-determined direction, ensuring that individual and collective performance is what it needs to be. But without a vision — something clear and attainable to accomplish — managers can do a very ***efficient*** job of maintaining the status quo, but not an ***effective*** job of achieving meaningful goals. As leadership gurus Warren Bennis and Burt Nanus wrote 20 years ago, "Managers do things right; leaders do the right things."

This is critical to effectively *Respond* to a situation. Without a clear vision of what we're trying to accomplish, our goals and priorities, or a common definition of success, we're likely to *React* to whatever is burning, urgent or feel-good in front of us at the moment. Leaders and effective youth coaches *Respond.*

A good youth coach must be ***both*** a leader and a manager to overcome the tremendous inertia in youth sports. Kids bring to my team a collection of behaviors, habits, beliefs, and expectations. Some of these might align with what I want to achieve and some won't. If I'm going to lead, I have to reinforce what I want more of and, in a positive and productive way, change those things that don't fit my approach. But if I don't lead, I'll end up managing to someone else's vision.

I see the inertia in Brandon's batting stance and swing. He's been taught to do things a certain way (or made it up himself) but I can see that he can't hit the inside pitch if the guy throws hard. Brandon simply can't get his hands through the swing fast enough based on his learned or natural swing. I can either manage around this or lead him to a new level of success.

I also see the inertia and need to lead in the work habits of how the kids play catch and warm up before games and practices. On the first day of practice I inherited everything they'd been taught, seen, or believed about warming up. It may be tough to change, especially in one practice. But the longer I let it go and manage around it, the inertia grows stronger. So if, in March, I see them jacking around, throwing sidearm, looping the ball over their partner's head and then lazily walking after the dropped throws, and I do nothing, then I'll be able to blame only myself in June. While it's never too late to change something that isn't right, I think of it in terms of wasted time . . . three months is a long time to be doing something wrong. Consider how much improvement is possible in that area and other facets of the game if I address it immediately when I see it.

As an assistant coach the last seven years I've always deferred to the head coach and his vision. I've followed his lead. Now I'm the one setting the vision. I have to lead. I have to set expectations. I have to establish the tone. We don't argue with umpires, we don't throw bats, we hustle on the field, etc. If I don't set in motion my own vision of what this team should be and how we should think and act then nobody will . . . at least not this year . . . but then I hand off a bunch of bad habits to the next coach who has to spend time correcting those things before he can teach them something new. That is a wasted opportunity. I must lead.

March 26

Reaction at the Scrimmage Tournament

I wasn't proud of my behavior at the scrimmage tournament we played in yesterday. These were a series of one-hour scrimmages that gave us the opportunity to simulate game situations and better assess the individual kids and team as a whole.

In the last scrimmage of the day we played the team for which I was an assistant coach last season. I'll admit I wanted to do well against those guys — the coaches are still my friends, but the competitive juices still flow, especially when bragging rights are on the line.

That competitive line of thinking contributed to my negative *Reaction.*

For some reason the tournament organizers had two 14-year-old kids umpiring our scrimmage. While I'm very much in favor of kids learning to be umpires, they should earn their stripes with younger kids — not their peers. These teenagers were very inexperienced and allowed the coaches on the other team to bully them into making calls in their favor.

Several times the four coaches would burst from the other dugout, loudly disputing a call. The umpires, wanting to avoid confrontation, would immediately change their ruling. They caved so quickly that play was never disrupted. It was almost like Pavlov's dogs . . . the other dugout would make noise and the umpire would reverse his call. More than a few times the kid at home plate even yelled "strike" after the catcher had already thrown the ball back to the pitcher.

In these situations I would venture, mostly innocently, from the dugout asking for an explanation. The umpire, who was shorter than four of my players, wouldn't answer my questions. It felt grossly unfair that he would listen to the other coaches, but not talk to me. I quickly became the one on the field, agitated and disrupting play; the other dugout, having gotten their way, was calm and agreeable. I got played, and played well.

Hello, rational mind? You there?

It was a scrimmage. We weren't keeping score. It didn't matter. I should have let it go. But I couldn't. I got sucked in, becoming angrier and angrier with each pitch to the point I could only focus on a few narrow things:

1. *The injustice of the situation. (Fairness is a personal hot button of mine.)*
2. *The other team was beating us at baseball.*
3. *The other team was using the umpires to win.*
4. *I really wanted to do well and make a good showing against my former mates . . . I wanted to prove we could compete with them.*
5. *I was determined to not let them beat me at baseball or the game they were playing with the umpires.*

As a result, I was really, really frustrated. I did a lot of yelling, ranting, and raving, and I did not set a good example of how to deal with umpires or tough situations. I wasn't the role model I wanted to be, and later I was embarrassed by my behavior. The game ceased to be fun for me, and I'm sure it was less fun for our kids. My actions shifted the game's focus from the players on the field to the coaches and umpire. I *Reacted.* I lost sight of what was most important — having fun, helping the kids learn, and being competitive.

I realize now I need to constantly be aware of the competitive juices and quickly tone them down when they begin to spike. Fortunately, I've got the whole season in front of me . . . each game will be an opportunity to practice what I learned yesterday.

March 28

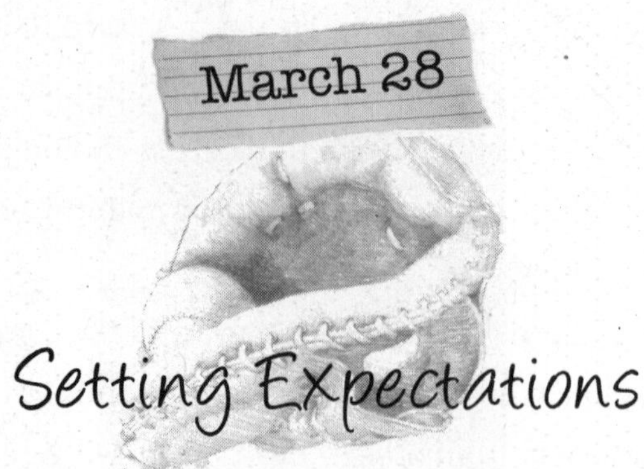

Setting Expectations

Tonight at practice I had the opportunity to further assert my role as a leader of the team and set expectations for the boys. Lackadaisical doesn't begin to describe how they warmed up at the beginning of practice. They made wild throws, gave little effort to catch bad tosses, and slowly trudged after the ball once it got by them. I watched for a while, giving instructions to individuals as I walked up and down the line, imploring them to take it more seriously. My suggestions, however, had little impact. They continued their conversations about school, girls, and video games (not in that order), looking only slightly better than the rag-tag talent at the local sand lot.

Having seen enough, I yelled, "All right guys, everybody in." I'm sure they were expecting practice to begin. Instead I decided we needed to be clear on how this new team of 11 players would warm up and prepare for practices and games.

"Guys, that was bad," I said once they gathered in a loose huddle. "We made terrible throws, we didn't catch the ball unless it was thrown right at us, and I saw almost no hustle." I paused as I looked into 11 sets of eyes.

"When you were younger, or playing at less competitive levels, you may have had different expectations or may have been taught different things. But now you're playing AAA," I explained.

"This is competitive baseball," I continued with a calm but stern tone. "It is important that you do everything with purpose and you do it fundamentally well. Our purpose is to get our arms loose and ready for practice, build arm strength, and reinforce good throwing mechanics."

I thought they'd be hanging their heads, having just been reprimanded. Surprisingly, though, they were focused and paying more attention than when I began my talk. "Let me be clear about what I expect from this team. We'll make good, strong, accurate throws to our partners. We'll actively move our feet and bodies to be in position to catch the ball. If it gets by us, two things will happen. The person who missed the ball will sprint after it and sprint back to position. The person making the bad throw will sprint to the other foul line and back. Each of you is old enough and good enough to do this right and do it well. This level of effort and performance sends a message to each other, and the other teams, that we belong at AAA."

I surveyed the group and saw a few heads nodding in agreement. "Okay guys, go back and warm up like a AAA team."

They ran out to their spots and it was 100 percent better. They were still talking and laughing, but the tone was different. I sensed pride coming from the team, something I haven't seen since the dramatic win that got us into AAA a couple of weeks ago. In the following 10 minutes there were only a few missed balls or bad throws. I was amazed! I didn't have to yell or get frustrated; they just went out and did it. I think they appreciated the structure, discipline, and higher expectations.

I can't believe it was that easy. I'm not naive enough to believe it will always be that effortless. There will be times nothing will work, and there will be instances where I'll have to reinforce expectations and dole out consequences to get the right behavior. Communicating clear expectations, however, is a good starting point.

While this experience will hopefully produce a lasting behavior change in those 11 players, I think it made a bigger impression on me. I better appreciate my responsibility and opportunity as the leader of this team.

March 29

React Mode Warning Sign #1 — Emotional

As I reflect on my behavior at the scrimmage tournament I realize I disregarded a warning sign of *React* mode: strong emotions.

Emotions are a neither good nor bad, they're simply a central part of being human. We can't get rid of them, nor should we try. In fact, if we did manage to expel them from our experience, our lives would likely fall apart. There's a great body of research in neuroscience that indicates we can't live a functional life without emotions. In his book *Descartes Error*, Antonio D'Amasio profiles several patients with damage to the part of the brain responsible for integrating emotions with rational thought. After their injuries, their lives fell apart, mainly because they couldn't make good decisions. D'Amasio's assertion is that emotions help push us in a direction towards one decision or another. Without a nudge, we humans make either no decisions or ones that are often self-destructive.

However, as important as emotions may be, we shouldn't act on them alone. That's the mistake I made the other night. I was acting on my frustration with the injustice of the situation, anger at the other coaches and umpire, and probably a fear of losing. I let those emotions run wild. At times it felt like a heavy train on a steep section of track — no control and in constant danger of a wreck. I didn't integrate those powerful feelings into my logical thought process or align them with my larger ideals and goals for the team. They were a very seductive narrow slice.

So as I think more clearly about making *Response* a habit, I must be careful not to act quickly on raw emotion. I must see them as a clear warning sign that I'm in *React* mode, collect myself, and try to integrate them with rational thinking.

As with so many things in baseball and life: simple . . . not easy.

Part III

April

Reacting to Robert's Bunt Defense

I blew it at practice tonight. I *Reacted* to Robert in a way that confused the kids and will require more work from me to correct. I was running about 20 minutes late from work and called Robert and asked him to hit infield practice until I got there. No big deal; we can always use 10 to15 minutes of extra practice on ground balls. My plan was to teach our basic bunt defense. It's a pretty simple strategy that as the kids get older and into high school other coaches will build upon.

When I arrived Robert had already started explaining his version of a bunt defense. As I walked out onto the field there were 11 kids staring blankly, listening to Robert detail what sounded to me like a very complicated scheme. It required every kid to memorize several different rules of what to do based on which side of an imaginary line the ball was hit, where the base runners were at the moment, and who was playing the defensive positions (some kids are faster than others). I was immediately confused but I thought it was just because I had gotten there late.

I was miffed that he had started this instruction — I had asked him to wait for me. And, I was surprised at how complicated his instructions were. That's partially my fault for not discussing it with him ahead of time and getting agreement on an approach. But I wasn't planning on him doing the instruction.

Anyway, I decided not to interrupt and contradict him in front of the kids. That would hurt his credibility and, understandably, make him angry. I hoped that once he was finished explaining I'd better understand his strategy and find a way to simplify it. However, I couldn't understand or simplify. Now I have confused kids and I'll need to spend another 15 to 20 minutes of valuable practice time changing things to my strategy. Dang — this is a setback.

At the time I was uncomfortable. I didn't like the fact that Robert didn't follow my directions, but I didn't want a confrontation, either. I know my personality is to avoid confrontation, and, in a situation like this, it's a weakness. I was also a little fearful that I didn't understand his instruction and that, not knowing all the facts, I'd look stupid in front of the kids if I got into a debate with him.

So I *Reacted* to the narrow pieces in front of me — the fear of looking foolish and the discomfort of confrontation. The larger ideals of **fun, learn,** and **compete** got shoved aside. Being confused isn't fun and learning the wrong things doesn't make you competitive. I lost sight of those team goals — or at least didn't act on their behalf when I had the chance. On the plus side, because I didn't embarrass Robert in front of the kids, I will be able to talk with him one-on-one and he shouldn't be defensive. However, I should have found a way to both teach the right thing and not alienate Robert — or at least err on the side of a *Response* that aligned more with our goals.

I *Reacted.* I should have been stronger. I should have led.

April 4

React Mode
Warning Sign #2 – Selfish

I've been thinking more about my *Reaction* the other day to Robert's bunt defense. I still don't quite understand his strategy, but I'm more concerned with my behavior at this point. I think another warning sign of *React* mode is being selfish. Ultimately, that's what I was.

I was selfishly protecting my fear of looking stupid and avoiding the discomfort of a confrontation. The selfishness short-circuited my ability to see the larger picture and *Respond* in a way to move the team forward.

When you strip everything away, being selfish is ego or "me" driven behavior to get pleasure or avoid pain. Selfishness puts the needs of the individual above those of the team, which often means we don't achieve larger goals and objectives. A sign of selfish behavior is rationalization . . . I'm sure Jimmy really does prefer to play outfield anyway . . . I'm cold and it's getting late so it's okay if Joey doesn't take batting practice tonight . . . it would be a lot of work to change the lineup card right now so Brian will have to hit last again this game . . .

This experience made me realize something important.

As coaches we give our time selflessly. But this generosity can hide selfish *Reactions*, even from ourselves. I was only slightly aware the other night that I was acting in my own self-interest — things happened quickly and they weren't unfolding the way I had planned. I made a snap decision on partial information, hoped for the best, and rode it to the bitter end.

I should have asked myself a quick question: "What's my motivation?"

If I had done that — and answered honestly — I would have acted differently. I might have seen several other options, including:

- Stopping the instruction and making a joke to change the tone and then saying, "Coach Robert's done a great job of explaining a lot of the 'why's' behind what we want. Here's another way of thinking about our bunt defense . . ." and gone into my strategy.
- Stopping the bunt discussion and do some more infield practice. "Okay, guys, let's put this into practice with some infield situations," and then after 5 to 10 minutes simulate some bunts and give my instruction, "Coach Robert's done a great job of explaining a lot of the 'why's' behind our approach to bunts. Here's another way of thinking about it . . ."
- Interrupting with, "Several of you look confused — I mean, more confused than normal (pause for laugh or groans). Here's another way of thinking about it . . ."
- Giving everyone a water break and taking a moment to discuss things with Robert. We could have come back from the break with a simpler explanation.

Those would have been good *Responses*. Instead, I was selfish. I *Reacted*. Next time I'll do a better job.

April 8

Sliding at Second – Part 1

We won a scrimmage the other day, which was our last tune up before the regular season starts. We looked pretty good and I got five kids time on the mound. With the season starting next week, we still have several things to improve. Our infield is rusty because, with all of the snow, we haven't been outside to take ground balls. We need to work on base running, getting good leads, and holding runners on base.

One other thing that is surprising me is that we had several kids, including Alan, who didn't slide at second or third base. Not only is this important to increase our chances of getting to the base, but it is also a safety issue. Kids on both teams can get hurt if they don't slide.

We've talked about it and spent a few minutes in practice going through proper technique. I'm sure they'll get better. Isn't it every kid's dream to slide safely into second or third? Growing up I always thought that was cool to get my uniform dirty (although Mom didn't think so). I mentioned that to Alan and he just shook his head and rolled his eyes.

We'll work on the sliding issue.

April 13

Book Review – Randomness and Yelling at Kids

I've been reading a good book about how the randomness of events impacts everyday life. It influences everything from political polls, wine tasting, corporate success, and school grades. Although the concept of randomness is steeped in math and probability, I'm glad there are very few numbers in the book (*The Drunkard's Walk: How Randomness Rules Our Lives*, by Leonard Mlodinow). I'm enjoying his discussion of the randomness of performance. The key concept is "regression towards the mean." The wisdom I'm gleaning is that yelling at players for mistakes doesn't improve their performance.

His rationale is that every player has a unique level of ability that translates to their own "average performance" — what you expect from John will be different than Joey. For example, John might make a catch seven out of 10 times while Joey's average performance level is to make that same play four of 10 times.

So if John makes an error, it is one of those three that you'd expect if you hit him 10 balls. The next one you hit him though, he is much more likely to catch because, on average, he makes it 70 percent of the time. So, says the author, it is math — not the sternness of the coach's voice — that makes the next play better.

Aberrations in results from a player's average ability, Mlodinow argues, are simply part of the randomness of life. And the underlying probability that caused the error in the first place is also pulling the player's performance back (regression) towards the average (mean), or expected performance, on the next chance.

He explains that many coaches get satisfaction for yelling and then seeing the player's performance improve on the next opportunity. So they quickly learn to yell at the kid to improve the performance. It appears to be simple cause and effect. It doesn't take long, nor do you have to be Pavlov, to make that your coaching style. What Mlodinow explains though, is that even by doing nothing, the kid's performance has a high probability of being better on the next play — he's likely to perform near his average.

The inverse is also true. Coaches tend to praise a player when he makes a great play and then are disappointed if on the next play he doesn't do it equally well. Again, it is probability that is pulling the player's performance back towards his average.

This concept of regression to the mean is not meant to minimize the role of a coach. Rather, it reinforces the need for good coaching and illustrates how difficult the job really is. If yelling worked, it would be easy to transform the Bad News Bears into a contender. Yelling is the easy way out . . . you get a small bump in performance, but the improvement is thanks to randomness, not the coach.

A good coach works on a slower timetable and requires a lot more patience. The tools he wields are instruction, positive reinforcement, and encouragement . . . these create a larger opportunity to improve the player's ability level over several practices or games.

Randomness and regression towards the mean should change the coach's focus from the result of the very next play to the longer-term development of skills. Our role is to help the player learn what they can from each experience in a productive and positive way, and build skills so that over time, a player's average performance level increases.

This means that every mistake is an instructional opportunity, not an excuse to scream. So we need a lot less yelling and more encouragement and instruction. This is what drives performance over the long haul of the season.

And, by the way, this mathematical analysis says nothing of stoking the kid's desire to play with encouragement, or dampening it through yelling.

This though does not mean to imply, though, that a coach can't or shouldn't, at opportune times, give a kid the verbal equivalent of a kick in the rear for a poor attitude, lack of effort, or recurring mental mistake. But those situations are the rarity versus the anguish over a botched play.

I'm taking several things from this book:

1. *Regression towards the mean is responsible for short-term variability in a player's performance.*
2. *Yelling at the player only diminishes his enjoyment, desire, and motivation to make the next play.*
3. *The goal of a coach is to help the player improve his average performance level — to become a better player for the long haul.*
4. *Instruction helps a player understand* ***how to improve****; encouragement makes him* ***want to improve****.*

The following two graphs illustrate these points.

Graph A: Jimmy

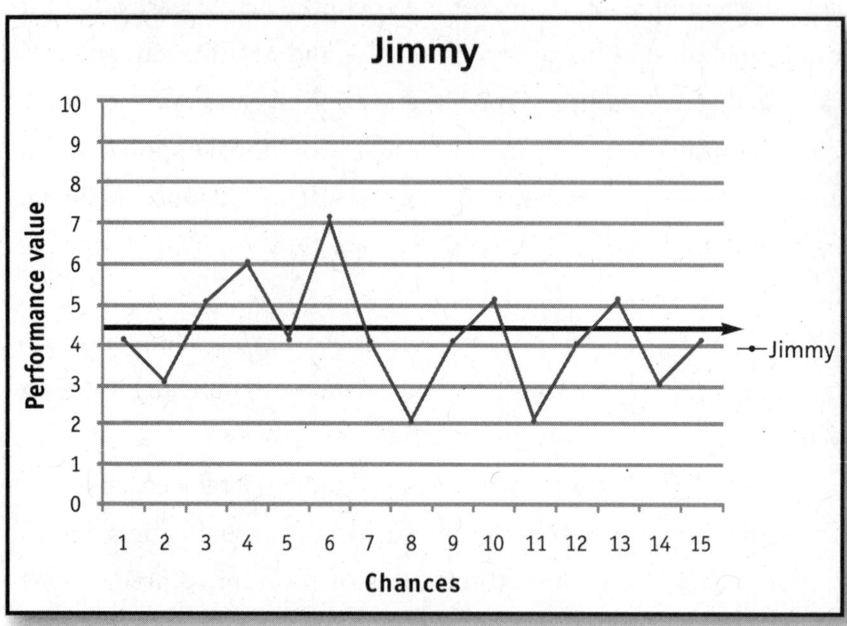

Here, Jimmy's performance mean (average) is about a 4.1 for fielding ground balls and making a strong, accurate throw to first base. He's had a couple of really good plays (for him), scoring a 6 on the fourth chance and a 7 on the sixth chance. His above average plays are usually followed by a lower score which is more reflective of his talent level. This is regression towards the mean. Similarly, bad plays (scores of 2 or 3) are usually followed by something better, again reflecting the average of Jimmy's ability.

If a coach yells at Jimmy for the score of 2 on the eighth chance, his score was likely going to go up anyway. The yelling simply makes Jimmy feel less good about himself, the coach, and the game. He's less happy to be on the field, more timid, and afraid to make a mistake.

Similarly, a coach might think he should never praise a kid ever again after heaping it on Jimmy for the 7 on the sixth chance and then seeing it plummet back down to his mean of a 4. That's randomness, not soft coaching. Coaches should continue to praise, they just shouldn't get frustrated if the kid doesn't do as well the next time. Think of it as an investment that fuels desire in the short term and improvement over the long term. The kids will improve with enough instruction, practice, and encouragement . . . yelling just stunts their growth.

Graph B: Dustin

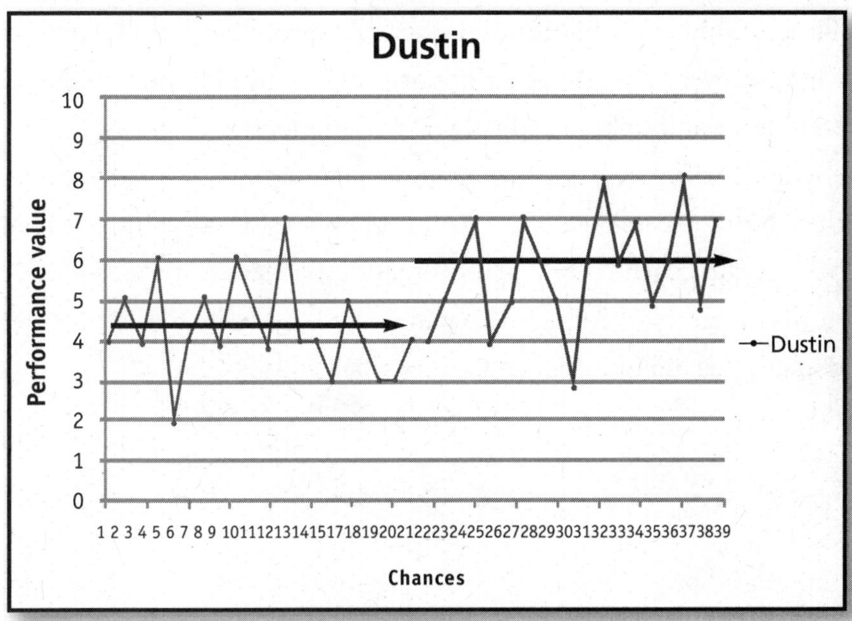

Dustin's performance is what we're striving for by providing instruction and encouragement. With a positive and constructive approach to Dustin's performance, his coach is keeping him excited and engaged in the game, making him want to do it again and again.

Dustin wants to listen to feedback, get more instruction, and he wants to perform.

Look at the trend this creates. For the first half of the graph (20 chances) his average performance is a 4.3. For the second half, the coach's instruction and encouragement have turned fertile ground into sweet fruit . . . the patience and encouragement enable the team to reap the benefits of a 6.0 performer. That's coaching.

Mlodinow's book, *The Drunkard's Walk*, reinforced the idea that, as a coach, I'll never be able to take the randomness completely out of performance. I have to be able to look at a larger part of the graph, a larger number of chances, and work to improve the overall trend. If I look at every mistake as an opportunity to give instruction, build confidence and stoke passion, then I make randomness an ally, not the enemy. I will wring improvement out of kids and I will add fuel to their burning passions for the game. I have to stop coaching one play behind and coach several plays (or games) ahead. Ultimately, I can impact what a player knows how to do and his desire to do it . . . the doing is then up to the kid and the baseball gods.

April 14

The Busy Day

Today was a demanding day and I earned a coaching stripe, at least in my own mind. I was so busy with organizing and administrative details I barely had time for my real job. Almost everything I did fell into the thankless category — most of it will go unnoticed by parents and players. And that's okay. If I do my job well, then everything runs smoothly, as you would hope and expect. If I'm not effective, then things fall through the cracks and a portion of the underlying complexity is revealed to all.

While they often thank me for my sweat, few have an appreciation for the effort that goes into planning and executing a practice, building a game lineup, registering and preparing for a tournament, fundraising, organizing a scrimmage, or buying equipment and uniforms. But every task I accomplished today was necessary … if I didn't follow through, parents and kids would have a bad experience because something was forgotten, poorly organized, or not thought through.

Individual tasks by themselves are usually manageable, but when they hit on the same day like today, the coaching job can, at best seem taxing, at worst, overwhelming. By the time I left for the field at 4:30 p.m.

I was exhausted. I had given a lot, but I hadn't provided any instruction or done one thing to help a kid improve.

It would be interesting for parents and kids to shadow their coach for a day. Here's what mine would have experienced today.

7:45 — 8:15 a.m.

While sipping a cup of coffee I entered our roster online for the tournament next weekend. This was slow and tedious; not only did I need to triple check names and birthdates, I had to alternate between brute force and gentle massage to get the cooperation of the antiquated Web site. I also sent out my fourth email to parents reminding them that I still need to get copies of birth certificates. It seems like a simple task, but I still have three who haven't followed through. Instead of sending individual emails to those three like I did last time, I sent a blanket plea to the whole team. I didn't name names but this strategy should create some well-deserved peer pressure — nobody likes to feel like a deadbeat.

8:53 — 9:03 a.m.

In between conference calls, I registered for a tournament next month. As a foreshadow to the way the rest of my day was going to go, this simple thing took a lot longer than it should have. The first time through I got 15 of the 16 numbers on my credit card correct . . . although that's a darn good batting average, it doesn't get you registered for a baseball tournament! On the second reading of the string of numbers I caught the mistake and corrected it. But by then the system had blanked out the card expiration date and gave me an error. I had to start all over.

9:05 — 9:09 a.m.

While waiting for a straggler to join my next conference call, I sent an email to the league asking for the insurance certificate to be faxed to the tournament director for this weekend's event. Our league needs a better process for this. For some reason, they can't give a copy of the certificate to individual coaches so that we can present it to the tournament director at check in for our first game. Instead we have to request that the league fax it, confirm that it was received, and sometimes re-request.

9:52 — 10:06 a.m.

Brandon's mom called me asking for guidance on buying a bat for his birthday. I explained that the length is measured in inches and the weight in ounces. That gives each bat a number, like a -7, which means it is seven inches longer than it weighs in ounces. We decided that a 32-inch with a -7 or -8 would be best for Brandon.

10:06 — 10:13 a.m.

I called the sporting goods store and talked to them about getting replacements for two jerseys. When they originally produced the shirts the numbers weren't applied correctly and they are wrinkled and bubbled. Not only do they look bad, I'm concerned the numbers will fall off after a few times through the washing machine. The store was helpful (after a long explanation) and said to bring the jerseys in this afternoon and they could repair or replace them on the spot. This is good news — we'll have them for the tournament games tomorrow. I sent emails to the two parents to see if they could bring the jerseys in today.

10:15 — 10:18 a.m.

I sent an email to coach Sam asking him to pick up the other dozen baseballs from the league office. We were supposed to get three to start the season, but they only had two for each team. They're now in and Sam said he'd pick them up.

10:18 — 10:27 a.m.

The sporting goods store called back and said they didn't have the right numbers and jerseys in stock — a box was labeled incorrectly. This is turning into quite the hassle. The store is rushing the order but won't have what they need until early next week. I sent another email to the two parents, this time saying not to worry about the uniforms today.

11:05 — 11:18 a.m.

I called Sam to get his thoughts on practice for tonight as well as the strategy for the tournament over the weekend. It's extremely valuable to have good coaches who can provide insight and listen while you bounce ideas. He had several good suggestions and reinforced a few things Robert mentioned when I talked to him yesterday. Time well spent.

11:20 — 11:35 a.m.

I developed the practice plan for tonight, a short session before the tournament tomorrow and Sunday. Unfortunately our practice time assigned by the league is on Friday evenings . . . not ideal, but at least we do get a field.

Tonight after warm-ups we're going to break into three groups. I want to work with four pitchers on their change up grips. They haven't seemed to master it yet, and I think 20 to 30 throws in the bullpen will get them on track. That will also give me the opportunity to see how each is doing with some of the tweaks we made to their mechanics. I'll know pretty quickly who has been working on it and who hasn't.

While I'm doing that, I'll have Robert hitting infield and working technique for staying down on ground balls. This is going to be an ongoing need for our kids — we are not a good fielding team yet. And I'll have Sam work with the outfielders on positioning themselves behind the fly ball and moving in on the catch. He'll also have them hit the cutoff man — that's another thing we have not yet mastered.

We'll then do a quick round of BP with me pitching, giving each kid six good swings. Robert will continue to hit ground balls to infielders in between pitches and Sam will give the on-deck hitter soft toss with wiffle balls. Practice will end with base-running and I'll discuss a few key messages about focus, intensity, and playing hard tomorrow in the tournament. It should be 90 minutes well spent and we'll be ready for the weekend.

12:10 — 12:35 p.m.

I'm eating my lunch and making the lineup for tomorrow's games. It's not easy to have each player get the right number of innings per game in the right positions at the right times. If I'm not careful, I can end up with a defensive lineup that can implode and give the other team a really big inning. A few errors up the middle or at first base and the game can turn ugly in a hurry. I usually try to have my best players at each position when the other team has the heart of their order up . . . I want our best against their best. This means I want the best defense in for the first inning for the top of their order. And I usually want our best defense planned out for the sixth inning so that if it is close, we have the best chance to win.

But if it is a slow-moving game, time may expire and the last inning might be the fifth . . . so do I put our best defense in for the fifth and sixth? If I do that, then I have to sacrifice something earlier in the game to get the kids playing the positions they want to, even though they aren't the best at those spots. But our philosophy is about giving each kid an opportunity, and if he doesn't get the chance to play his position in a game, he's not going to get better (or have fun, or learn, etc.). I try to rotate it so that the same kids aren't sitting out at the start of the game every time. This "simple" exercise of filling out the lineup card can quickly turn into one of those college-level matrix/logic tests . . .

The batting order isn't easy either. Some kids really don't care what spot in the order they hit. Others though, prefer the challenge of having it based on their performance. If they hit well, they want to move up; if they don't they're okay with moving down. Some can't handle hitting at the bottom very well. I try to mix it around, but still stack our best hitters in the middle to give us a chance to score each time they come up, which is about every-other inning. It usually takes me a good 15 minutes to plan the lineup so that we accomplish everything we need to.

1:10 — 1:20 p.m.

After searching through my email for several minutes I finally found the phone number of the coach of the Cougars, a majors team, and called him to schedule a scrimmage for next week. A controlled scrimmage is a good way to get game-like experience for the kids while having the opportunity to stop play momentarily and give instruction. This majors team has lost their first two games after jumping up from AAA last season. Even though they're probably a better team than we are right now, we'll both get something valuable from the scrimmage.

We'll be challenged by better competition, which helps us improve early in the season. They'll get some much-needed success and confidence playing against us. I need to call another coach and see if I can swap practice times so that we can scrimmage on our field at 5:00 p.m. rather than our scheduled 6:30 - 8:00 p.m. timeslot.

1:43 — 2:02 p.m.

It took three phone calls to get a coach that would swap practice times with me on Wednesday for the scrimmage. I sent an email to the Cougars to confirm Wednesday at 5 p.m. I also sent an email to the two moms who are organizing the team's social event next weekend. I had a few ideas that might make for a better parent meeting. Fortunately, the moms are really on top of things and I was able to delegate the food and most of the activity planning to them. But we'll have 40 people over at the Thompson's and we need to make sure we've thought through the details.

2:56 — 3:03 p.m.

Tyler's mom called to let me know he came home sick from school today with a high fever. He's out for practice tonight and probably the games tomorrow. She said if he recovers she'll bring Tyler to the second game, but most likely he will be out all day. We'll just hope he's better by Sunday. Either way I have to now completely redo my lineup for the game in the morning. I'll have to do it tonight because I have to participate in a conference call for work that started three minutes ago . . . oops!

3:32 — 3:39 p.m.

When it rains, it pours. I checked voicemail and Robert said he's going to be late to practice if he makes it at all. He got called into a late meeting and doesn't expect to be there until the last 30 minutes of practice. I have to revise my practice plan because it means two coaches rather than three. I'll have Sam hit infield but that means nobody hitting fly balls . . . I hope a qualified dad will be there. If so, I will proceed with the original plan and modify the outfield drill according to the dad's competence level. If not I will either sacrifice some of the instruction with the pitchers or the outfielders. I could also have Sam throw batting practice while I work with pitchers. I have two viable options and will see what feels right when I get there.

3:45 — 3:50 p.m.

I called the tournament director and they just received the fax from our league office verifying the insurance. Nothing like getting it done at the last minute! I forgot to email the team mom and have her identify a few restaurants in the area of the park for tomorrow's games. Rats! I banged out a quick email and I hoped she'd get it before leaving work. Our first game is at 9 a.m. and the second one is at 1 p.m. so we'll need a quick lunch option that is close by. We have to think that through before we get there . . . experience says it is a mess if you try to wing it for food, especially in an unfamiliar town and hungry 12-year-olds clamoring for chow. I better call her on the drive to the field for practice to make sure we're covered.

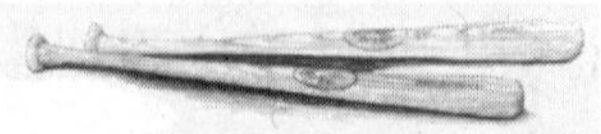

When you add it all up, I spent about 178 minutes on baseball-related activities. That's three hours, but doesn't count the loss in job productivity from jumping back and forth between projects. Not all days are this busy, but some are. Some include more difficult conversations with parents about playing time, or more lengthy discussions with coaches. I spent an additional 135 minutes driving to and from the field and running practice.

Five hours and 15 minutes . . . all volunteer. The kids are worth it . . . but I AM tired!

April 20

The Grand Slam

Alan was pitching in the tournament last weekend and worked himself into a jam in the second inning. He'd given up three runs and then loaded the bases with a hit and two walks. The other team's best hitter stepped up and hit Alan's first pitch over the left-centerfield fence for a grand slam homerun. That made it 7 - 0.

I was impressed by Alan's ability to bounce back from that gopher ball. He had a smile on his face; he knew he'd been beaten. I appreciated that he was both humble and still in a good emotional place. I kept him in the game because he still seemed to have a good attitude. His pitch count was low and I wanted to see how he would *Respond.* He struck out the next kid, but the catcher dropped the third strike and the batter ran to first. The catcher made an awful throw, way over the first baseman's head and into right field. The batter ended up on second base. Alan became distraught and the good attitude quickly evaporated into frustration.

So I marched out to the mound, took the ball and put him at third base. As Steve took his warm up pitches, I went over and talked to Alan. He was still fuming. "It's no fun when people can't catch or throw the ball," he spewed. "We're losing and I get a strikeout and we can't even get an out."

It was uncharacteristic of Alan to talk badly of his teammates. He usually was able to overlook miscues. And, I thought his anger was a bit misplaced . . . the dropped ball didn't cause the first seven runs. I've wanted Alan, and all the kids, to take more personal accountability for their actions on and off the field. Gently, I tried to put things in perspective.

"Alan, buddy, you know your fielders might all be saying the same thing after you walk two batters and then give up a home run," I explained in a soft and supportive voice. "They don't like losing if they don't even get a chance to touch the ball. You have to take responsibility for what you can do and not blame your teammates."

Mistake.

The moment was much too fragile. Alan burst into tears. Nice move, coach. Great. Way to go, dad. Go ahead, kick your 12-year-old when he's down.

I put my arm around him and said, "Hey come on now. You've got to shake this off. Games like this are going to happen. You're going to give up homeruns like that. All of us do. You have to learn how to accept it, learn from it, and move on."

He looked at me like I clearly didn't understand his despair. At 12 he's still under the notion that I walked on water as a player. I wanted to comfort him, but also reinforce the fact that I, too, had been in those lonely shoes, helplessly watching your pitch sail effortlessly over the fence.

Steve still had a few warm up pitches left so I quickly recounted my experience pitching in an American Legion state playoffs game after graduating from high school. I started the quarterfinal game and managed to load the bases and give up a grand slam homerun. I explained to Alan that not only did it travel over 400 feet, I had the additional embarrassment of the game being broadcast on radio. I hoped it would comfort him to know everybody in the stadium and the entire radio listening audience knew I just given up a colossal grand slam homerun. This seemed to calm Alan a bit, and so I trotted back to the dugout.

Then, yesterday, I heard Alan and my dad laughing as they were coming upstairs. I poked my head out of my office just in time to hear my dad say, "Yeah, not only did I see it leave the park, but I also listened to the radio announcer describe it." And they broke into laughter again.

I gave my dad a crusty look and retreated back to my office. At least Alan has recovered.

April 23

Getting Tossed

I got ejected from the game last night and I really hope that this is the low point of the season. I felt absolutely awful getting tossed. It was embarrassing and I felt that I let down the team and the parents. Honestly though, I don't think I deserved to have been thrown out. But that is beside the point — the umpire is really the only one that gets to vote on that issue. And like other judgment calls, you don't have to agree with them, but you do have to respect them … and live with them.

Because my journal is about the only place where I truly get to lay out the full facts of the case, I'd like to submit the following testimony and evidence for the defense.

It all happened in the bottom of the first inning. Alan was on first with one out and Nick hit a ground ball to the second baseman. Alan ran on the crack of the bat and as he got about 15 feet from second base, the shortstop caught the throw and stepped on the bag for a force play. Alan was out and he stopped running. The shortstop didn't make the throw to first because he saw that there would no play — Nick was already crossing the base. However, the umpire ruled that it was interference on Alan because he did not slide. As a result, he called Nick out too … a double play that ended the inning.

I was in disbelief. How could he have made that call? I paused for a moment to make sure I understood what just happened to our offensive threat. The flood of opposing players from the other team passing me by on the way to their dugout confirmed that, yes, it was an inning-ending double play. I started walking from the third base coaching box, approaching the umpire trying to get an explanation of what he had ruled and why. The base umpire had made his call from just behind the pitching mound and was heading toward the home plate umpire, as they often talk between innings.

Although frustrated, I tried to remain calm and asked the umpire what he had ruled.

"The runner has to slide, coach," the umpire said bluntly and started to look away, showing no interest in having the discussion he knew was about to take place.

I tried to explain that Alan was fifteen feet from the bag and that it would have been ridiculous for him to have to slide in that situation, he'd be lying on the ground in the middle of the field. Both umpires stood arms crossed staring into center field, not at all responsive to what I was saying. But that didn't stop me. Despite the fact that my argument was falling on deaf ears, I raised my voice a bit and continued my line of reasoning.

"He would have to start his slide before he knew if there was even going to be a play at second base," I explained, pointing towards the infield. My opening argument hadn't fazed these two judges, so I decided to start my cross-examination. "What if the second baseman had the ball go through his legs into the outfield? My base runner wouldn't see that because it would happen behind him. But he'd have to anticipate that he was going to field it and throw to second. In this case he should start his slide, but he'll look very foolish sliding when the ball is in the outfield."

On a roll, at least in my own mind, I continued. "And if he has to slide so far from the base, what happens of the shortstop drops the throw from the second baseman? Then my guy is lying on the ground, helpless, fifteen feet from the base, while the guy who drops the ball picks it up and tags the base."

All I got from the umpire was, "He's got to slide, coach."

Obviously, in legal terms, he was being non-responsive. Should I ask to treat him as a hostile witness? That, unfortunately, would come soon enough.

Now I will concede that I had raised my voice a bit, but according to reliable witnesses (parents) deposed after the game, I still was not loud or obnoxious. Nor was I insulting, condescending, or using profanity. Oblivious to where this was heading, I decided to go for the closing argument and rest my case.

"Come, on," I pleaded, "there was no play anyway. My batter beat that out. There's no way he doubles him up at first."

For the first time I got something besides the Easter Island stone face from this guy. "He has to slide, coach. That's the rule," he said, glaring at me, clearly with no appetite for debate.

I shook my head in disbelief and as I turned to towards my dugout said, "Unbelievable."

I knew I was upset and a bit animated, but didn't believe I had crossed the line. As I walked back to my team, Alan asked, "So what am I supposed to do at second?"

Tyler added, "Do we always have to slide there, coach?"

I realized I had no consistent instruction to give my team. Given the umpire's ruling, I really didn't know how to answer either question. So I whirled around to ask for clarification from the umpires.

Upon approach I said, "Look, I'm not arguing the call, I just want to know what to tell my kids what to do at second. Do they always have to slide?"

The base umpire looked at me and barked, "You're done here coach," and quickly gestured with his index finger, signaling me, I thought, to return to the dugout.

Encouraged by finally getting a response from the guy, I said, "No, I'm not arguing the call. I just want to know what to tell my kids to do in that situation."

He took two steps towards me and with more anger said, "You're done here coach," and again pointed towards the dugout.

I can take a hint. I said "okay," and thought I'd address it with him in the later innings after we'd both had a chance to cool off and think it through. I started talking to coach Sam in front of our dugout and then heard the umpire behind me, "Get off the field coach or I will start tossing your assistant coaches, too," he growled.

Surprised, I turned around. The reality of his words started to sink in. I looked at him with an uncomfortable smile on my face and a growing pain in my gut. "Oh, you threw me out of the game?" I asked, now fully aware of what had just transpired.

And to think some people say I can be dense at times.

"Get off the field now!" was a clear enough answer for me. I gathered my gear and sat in the stands next to our dugout. After the first few pitches of the next inning some of the parents asked why I was sitting with them, not realizing that I'd been ejected. There had been no clues at the scene of the crime, like a commotion, yelling, antics, confrontation or prolonged argument.

"Wow! You didn't even get your money's worth," one said.

Eventually the umpire asked me to leave the bleachers and I watched the rest of the game from the front seat of my car. That was the worst part of the whole thing … having to sit in the silence and ponder my behavior.

Alone in the dark, I wished I had done things differently. Several things rattled through my head, each making me more and more embarrassed and disappointed in my behavior.

1. ***I am supposed to be a role model.*** Role models handle adversity and difficult situations with grace and tact. They keep the big picture in mind and try to show kids how to work with challenging people and situations. I felt I had damaged my credibility, and perhaps my ability to be a positive role model, especially this early in the season.
2. ***Behavior unbecoming.*** While I wasn't a raving lunatic out there, obviously at least one person thought my behavior wasn't consistent with the expectations for youth sports. As a coach I now live with a rap sheet that includes being ejected from a game. There's no going back on that one.
3. ***Respect of the kids.*** I was concerned that I might lose the respect of the team. Respect of 12-year-olds, like any age, is earned because you know what you are doing and don't do stupid things.
4. ***Respect of the parents.*** Nobody wants their kid playing for a volatile hothead . . . will they see me as one? I don't think so, but now I've raised a few eyebrows and am less likely to get the benefit of the doubt in the future.
5. ***I have to miss the next game.*** The league has a rule that if you get ejected from a game, you have to sit out the next one too. We play our cross-town rivals, a team for which I was an assistant coach a few years ago. I'll have to watch from the stands. And if I get ejected from another game I'm out for the season.

6. ***Behavior expectations.*** I like to lead by example. Now that I've been tossed, I'll have the "Do as I say, not as I do" issue to deal with. I'll have to reset expectations with the kids at the next game. Will they now think that arguing with umpires is acceptable?

I also thought about how I could have prevented the incident. I kept asking myself how I would avoid that slippery slope and walk away before it gets out of hand. This is a tough point to find in the heat of the moment.

I realize that the line is different for every umpire and some are too tolerant. Aggressive coaches push around these well-intentioned folks. Other umpires have a very short fuse and quick temper. I've heard that some have contests with each other to see how many coaches they can eject during the season. Although I think I may have stumbled onto the latter, I still should not have done what I did.

After the game I apologized to the umpire and told him that the whole thing was my fault. I explained that I didn't realize I had been that agitated and that I was sorry. I think he felt he pulled the trigger a bit early and said he appreciated that I was apologizing. "Since you said you were sorry, I'm not going to report you to the league," he said. "You can coach your next game."

Those were magic words! I said thanks and left quickly before I could say anything stupid and change his mind. I dashed over to my team, who had gathered in the grass behind the bleachers, and I apologized to them and to the parents. It is not a fun thing to have to admit a major mistake to parents and players, especially one that involves lack of judgment and restraint. I'd rather make a major baseball blunder, like getting a runner thrown out at the plate, try to steal in an inappropriate time, or call for the cleanup hitter to bunt on a 3 - 0 count. In my book, all of those are more forgivable than losing your cool in front of kids, parents, and opposing teams.

Bev made a good point to Alan in the car on the drive home about owning mistakes. She said that because I had accepted responsibility, the umpire was forgiving. "When you do something stupid," she explained, "accept responsibility and move on. Don't make your bad behavior worse by arguing about it. People will forgive stupidity and the ridiculous things you might do, ***like your dad did tonight*** (her emphasis . . . she even turned her head towards me and paused with a scowl for dramatic effect), but only if you admit to them. So if you ever do something that incredibly foolish and dim-witted, own it." It was a good lesson for him, but I have to admit I felt all six tires rumble over my back as Bev tossed me under the bus . . .

As we were getting ready for bed that night, I finally had a chance to talk to Bev about it. I was trying to put things in perspective, and with my male ego reeling a bit, I was fishing for some support and perhaps even a little sympathy from my wife.

"You know that in all the years that I've played through high school and into college, all the years that I've played adult softball and baseball, and all the years I've coached Alan's baseball and basketball teams I've never been ejected from a game," I said, feeling good about that record and regaining a bit of pride.

I continued, "There are times where I admit that I probably should have been tossed, but I never have been ejected from a game. Not once."

Bev paused for a moment and, as if she'd been thinking it the whole time, said, "Well I'm glad you waited until you were in a role model situation to do it."

I swallowed what remaining pride I had and slinked off to bed.

April 24

Sliding at Second – Part 2

I'm starting to become concerned about the kids not sliding at bases. The play that triggered me getting ejected the other night was a slide — or lack thereof — at second base. I will grant Alan a pass on that one because he was 15 feet from the bag, but I see a reluctance of many of the kids to get down on close plays at the bases. It seems like there are far too many close plays where they come in standing up. If there is a positive side to me being thrown out of a game, maybe it will make an impression and reinforce the need to slide. We'll see.

April 25

Generation Why

Okay, so you don't have to read very far in the business literature to see that there are critical differences between the current generation and the ones that came before. Millennials, or members of Generation Y as they're sometimes called, have different expectations of just about everything. They question more, need instant gratification, expect their parents to bail them out of any uncomfortable situation, desire a relationship before they'll engage, and demand an explanation before they'll act. And, sadly, communication is electronic-driven.

I deal with this constantly in the workplace, but I'd like to believe I can hide from it on the baseball field.

Okay . . . I know, I know . . . an impossible dream of a Gen X'er. But I'm adamant that there are certain lines that shouldn't be crossed. Baseball, after all, is a sacred institution and, admittedly, I am a bit of a purist when it comes to the game . . .

I was talking to my coaching friend Marty the other day and he told me a story that made my skin crawl. During a game a couple of weeks ago Marty was trying to get his right fielder to move four or five steps towards centerfield. He was yelling and waving his arms, doing everything short of sending smoke signals from the third base dugout. Jeffery, though, was oblivious.

Jeffery's dad, a doting, if not engaged, Gen X parent, was on top of things. He'd been watching Marty wave, yell, jump, and gyrate. In a helpful tone, he asked the coach through the chain-link fence, "Marty, are you trying to get Jeffery's attention?"

Exasperated, Marty sighed, silently gestured several times toward the outfield with both hands, and then said, as politely as possible, something to the effect that, it wasn't necessary for his right fielder to hug the foul line.

Dad said he'd take care of it and whipped out his Blackberry. With only a few nimble keystrokes he'd dialed Jeffery's number and had the phone to his ear, ready to give instructions. Testifying to the exceptional cell network coverage at this field, in less than six seconds Jeffery turned his head down and to the right, reached into his back pocket and pulled out his cell phone.

Dad said, "Yeah, Jeff hang on," turned his head to Marty and said, "Five to the right, correct?"

Marty's jaw hit the dugout floor as he stared into the distance. Disbelieving the scene in which he was now an integral participant, the only reply Marty could muster was to slowly nod his head up and down.

Marty found dad's final words especially stinging, "Good job, son. Proud of you."

Jeffery quickly took the five steps to his right.

Wounded, Marty staggered backwards, balanced himself against the chain link with his left hand, and slowly sat on the bench. Sadly, I don't think he'll ever be quite the same man.

Our game is changing.

Flashback — Luis Sliding at Third

I've been thinking about the book on randomness and the idea that yelling at the kids doesn't improve performance. After a kid makes a play that is below his average (boots a ground ball), the concept of "regression towards the mean" insists that his next performance will be better than the last — closer to his average. A better *Response* from the coach is to offer encouragement and instruction so that the enthusiasm for the game stays high and the skill level improves. Yelling accomplishes neither.

After reading that part of the book, I'm flashing back to last season and a play that illustrates it perfectly.

Luis was a slightly above average player on the team, and did a lot of small things really well. He'd round the bases aggressively and take an extra base if the fielders bobbled the ball. He always stayed down on ground balls and his throws were fundamentally sound — a good arm motion and follow through to his target. The way he carried his bat and his body said, "I'm a hitter," and Luis had a good eye for the strike zone, which meant he rarely stuck out. A nice, quiet kid, he was always hustling and looking for ways to improve.

In this game we were behind by two runs in the third inning and Luis lined a double into right center with nobody out. Standing proudly on second base, the coach gave him the steal sign and he broke for third on the first pitch. He got a great jump, ran hard, and started a foot-first slide, approaching the outfield side of the bag so that the third baseman would have to move his glove farther to make a tag. It was a beautiful slide, just ahead of the ball reaching the bag — he had beaten the throw.

Unfortunately, though, Luis started his slide one step too late . . . his momentum carried him past the base by about a foot. He tried desperately to grab third base as he zoomed by, but lost his grip and the third baseman easily tagged him out. Yep, it was a rally killer. Instead of runner on third with nobody out, we had bases empty with one out. Dang.

The third base coach was frustrated. Bending over with hands on his knees, he dropped his head in disgust. While Luis slowly stood up and started dusting himself off, the coach exploded.

"Luis! What were you thinking?" he yelled loud enough for most spectators to hear. "That's awful. You killed our rally. You have to learn to stop at the base. We've told you since you were five years old that you cannot run past third base. You're killing me!"

In a matter of 10 seconds, Luis transformed from a tall and confident 11-year-old baseball player to a shamed, hunched over five-year-old troublemaker that had just been sent to his room without dinner. Before that play, he had been standing on second base, proud and perhaps even a bit cocky that he'd done a great thing for the team. Now he was trudging back to the dugout, head hanging and emotions in the dumps.

He slowly removed his helmet and let it drop to the ground by the stack of bats. He took a few more steps and sat down on the end of the bench, head down, dejected and staring at the cement floor. The other players avoided him as if he were radioactive. Concerned that the coach might yell at them too for associating with such a screw-up, they looked out at the field, quietly hoping they wouldn't do something equally deserving of a verbal berating.

I let the mood hang in the dugout for about a minute to allow the reality of what just happened sink in for Luis. I then got up from my spot in the middle of the bench, walked over and sat down next to him. I was silent and Luis continued to stare at the floor, not yet acknowledging my presence.

I put my arm around him and said softly, "Luis, you know what you did there, don't you?"

He was bracing for more abuse. "Yeah, coach. I started my slide too late."

"Well, yeah, there was that," I conceded. "But that's not what caught my eye and got me excited."

He slowly turned his head and looked up at me, a bit puzzled. He wasn't sure if I was serious or about to pull the rug out from underneath him and start yelling.

"What I saw was really good baseball," I said.

Luis thought I was toying with him, but went along anyway. "What do you mean coach?" he asked, hoping his growing interest in the conversation wouldn't backfire.

"Well, we were down by two runs and our team needed a spark — something to get us going, right?" I asked.

He hesitated a moment and said, "Well, yeah."

"I saw a good hitter get up to the plate, work the pitcher and then slap a solid hit into the outfield," I explained. "I saw you stay back on the pitch like we've talked about in batting practice. I saw you run hard all the way and stretch it to a double. I saw you smile at second base and

I heard this dugout erupt in cheers. In fact, Luis, I cheered too. I was right here in the middle of it, man. Your teammates were jazzed."

About this time a couple of Luis's friends came over and stood in front of him.

"Yeah, it was a great hit, Luis," said Cory.

"In fact, Pete was so excited he knocked over all of the bats." I said, pointing to the disorganized pile by the dugout entrance.

"Way to go, Pete, you klutz," joked Mark.

I turned back to Luis, "I then saw you look to the coach for a signal, take a good aggressive lead off of second and get a great jump on the pitcher. You had three steps before he released the ball. You ran hard and your slide was fundamentally very well done. Your leg was straight and your foot pointed. You slid to the outside part of the bag. That's perfect," I said, nodding my head.

Luis was now smiling, eyes beaming with pride while listening to this Joe Buck-like play-by-play praise of his performance.

"Now we all know you started the slide just one step too late. You should start it about eight or 10 feet away — that's about 2 body lengths. You slid past because you were only about five feet away when you started. You're not going to do that next time, are you?"

"No way, coach. I know what to do," he said with swagger returning to his voice and posture.

"That's what I thought," I concluded. "Now go get your teammates fired up and lets win this game."

Luis bounced off the bench and started yelling encouragement to the hitter. His teammates sensed it was okay to make noise again and the dugout was now full of energy. Later in the game Luis hit another double that drove in two runs to tie the game. He didn't try to steal third, but I'm willing to bet that if he did, he would have done it perfectly.

No matter what, Luis probably would have made a better slide on his next attempt. He's good enough that he doesn't normally make mistakes like that. His average performance is pretty high. His next slide will likely "regress to the mean" — probability dictates that it should improve to be closer to his average ability.

So as a coach you have three choices to deal with a situation like Luis over-sliding third base.

1. ***Yell.*** It might make you feel better as you're doing it to vent the frustration, and it does bring clarity to your expectations, but that's classic *React* mode behavior. Yelling only served to destroy Luis's confidence and ability to enjoy the game. Without those, he's much less likely to get a hit next time up and more likely to boot a ground ball in the field.
2. ***Say nothing.*** This is better than yelling, but Luis would still have a lot of self-doubt and it may take him a while to get back into the swing of the game. The silent treatment also misses an opportunity to reinforce the correct way to perform a slide. Certainly you've told the 12-year-old before . . . but that doesn't guarantee that he knows it.
3. ***Give instruction and encouragement.*** This gets him back into the fun zone of baseball much faster. With encouragement and instruction, he has confidence, passion and enthusiasm working for him — powerful tools no matter the age or activity.

Part IV

May

May 1

The Value of Instruction

I was out at the ball field about 15 minutes early for practice last night. It occurred to me that during the course of the season I get to observe many coaches working with kids of different ages and abilities. This idle time waiting for them to vacate the field is a good opportunity to calibrate against what other coaches do and reflect on my own techniques.

As I thought about it, I'm surprised at the lack of instruction that happens in practices and games. I'm guilty of it too — we get caught up in the heat of the moment and miss a valuable coaching opportunity. It's *Respond* vs. *React* in action I suppose, but it is something I should always be aware of and work to improve.

I have noticed that instruction, or perhaps better described as direction, from coaches often falls into one of three categories:

1. Scream at a kid for not doing WHAT is needed. "*You have to make that catch!!*" or "*You can't walk any more batters!*" It is after the fact . . . too late to do any good in this situation.

2. Yell at them about WHAT is needed. "*Get an out, infield!*" "*You have to put the ball in play!*" Direction for this situation, but often hollow and meaningless because there is no instruction or context.

3. Appropriately EXPLAIN to them HOW to do WHAT is needed and explain WHY this is important (the benefits to individual and team performance). Yes, this takes more time, but the dividends are huge for this investment in instruction.

I've noticed with a couple of kids on my team I tend to be more in the category 1 or category 2 areas too often. I assume they've already had the category 3 instruction and are simply not focused — or willing — to execute the plays. So I'm frustrated with their lack of effort and their performance.

This is a bad assumption on my part. In sports the HOWs are the fundamentals. They are essential to consistent, long-term success. If the kids don't understand the correct HOW, then it is the coach's fault. And kids are more likely to execute the HOW if they understand WHY they need to do it that way. At that point the WHAT becomes a matter of execution, and at times luck. (The ball hit a rock and bounced over the shortstop's head, even though he broke on the ball, charged hard and was in proper position to make the play.)

As I sat in the bleachers waiting for our turn on the field, I thought about these categories and had to accept the fact that the mistakes I see other coaches make are some of the same ones I do too. I just don't realize I'm doing it at the time.

In our last practice I committed a category 2 instruction with Tyler in centerfield. I was hitting infield/outfield and working on situations with the kids. He misplayed a ball hit to his right and it got by him, rolling most of the way to the fence. I hustled out to near second base so I wouldn't have to yell.

"Tyler, you have to take a better angle at the ball. You're letting some of them get by you that you should cut off and you're letting others drop in front of you that you should catch. Take better angles," I directed. He nodded and replied dutifully, "Okay, coach."

But what did I really tell Tyler? What help was I? Obviously he wasn't **trying** to let the ball get to the fence. He had run hard at the ball. He was trying to make the play. He ran just fast enough in the wrong direction to miss it. What I should have done was to review the instruction on how to better read the flight of the ball and make a snap decision on which one to dive for and which one to let bounce. He needed further instruction on taking a quick drop step on a ball hit in the gap and then to sprint to a spot. This would have taken less than two minutes and been good for the entire team to hear — and it would have told him HOW to do it right. I should have followed it up with the WHY: both techniques will make more outs and prevent runners from taking extra bases. With that instruction, several more opportunities on fly balls and encouragement, Tyler would get it. Instead he got the redundant message of "catch the ball" with no better idea of how to get that done.

I also thought about a situation where the category 1 or 2 can be on a positive play but the coach's statement adds little or no value for the player. In our last game Nick made a great play at third base. I yelled simply, "Nice play Nick, way to go!" At some level I'm sure my praise felt good, but he may not have been sure what he did right. I should have taken him aside after the third out, praised him again and said, "Nice play. You did a great job of attacking the ball. That's exactly what we've been talking about. You stayed low after you fielded it, stepped toward first base and made a good, strong, accurate throw. You even followed through for another step or two. That was perfect, Nick."

As for how coaches should apply these three categories in games and practice, yelling probably doesn't help at all, but, if done well, category 1 or 2 direction can support category 3 instruction. "*Tom, just like practice yesterday. The play is at first; remember we just need an out in this situation. We're up four runs and we'll trade an out for a run at this point.*"

Category 3 can be more difficult in a game because of the flow of play, but there are plenty of coachable moments in the dugout in between innings or even during a quick mound visit to talk to the pitcher and infielders.

This concept is also true for adults. I think about my work environment . . . does my job have more meaning and am I able to perform better when I know HOW to do something and WHY it is important . . . or do I just want the drill sergeant to scream more about the WHAT that needs to be done? Which fuels my passion for my job? Which pushes me to go above and beyond? Which makes me want to get out of bed and get to work early . . . and which makes me want to dust off my resume?

The WHAT only becomes important if kids understand both the HOW and WHY behind it. They become problem solvers rather than doers.

As the manager in the movie *Bull Durham* said, "Baseball is a simple game. You throw the ball; you catch the ball; you hit the ball."

Our job as coaches is to help the kids understand the complexity of how, when, and why they should do those simple things.

May 2

The Psychological Pain of Underperformance

This title sounds like something you'd find in a professional journal for psychiatrists. And I have to admit that when the team performs far below their capability, it sounds very appealing to lie down on the couch and get some professional help.

I have to continually remind myself that all teams at some point during the season will underperform. Every team, including the invincible 1927 Yankees, has at least a few games like this each season. There are many reasons, or at least explanations, for this but none totally alleviate the pain and frustration a coach feels watching his team play at a level far below what they've shown they can achieve.

That's been the Yellow Jackets' experience over the last week or so. Starting with the weekend tournament and carrying over to the two league games this week, we've played poorly, losing five games to average-quality teams.

During this stretch we've made physical errors, mental errors, botched fundamentals, failed to hustle, been lazy, and shown indifference. At times I've wondered if the kids really wanted to be out there playing baseball. They seem excited before the game and somewhat disappointed after the loss, but it's like they expect to press the reset button and restart their X-box game. I'm sure they realize it doesn't work that way . . . but after the last week I'm going to stop assuming I know what goes through the mind of a 12-year-old.

I'm not so worried about the result of five tallies in the loss column, rather I'm concerned with the lack of spirit or engagement when things start to go bad. Nobody seems willing to step up and make a play or otherwise rally their teammates with encouragement. Despite what cheerleading I might do, they seem content to quietly slide into what they believe is an inevitable loss. It's self-fulfilling. Perhaps that's what characterizes a slump, but I'm having a tough time bringing them out of that frame of mind.

And I've tried many things. I've reasoned with them, explaining the different competitive advantages they have at the time, and how effort will lead to victory. I've tried instruction, giving them specific tasks to do in the field or at the plate (like tell them before the pitch where the play will be), to be aggressive and hit the first strike they see, or move up in the box against a slower pitcher. I've re-explained my expectations and how they aren't meeting them. I've attempted joking with them, laughing about their lack of enthusiasm hoping they'll see it in a different way and change. I've juggled the lineup, both at the plate and in the field.

As this pile of miscues continues to grow it releases the deeper emotional desire to yell and scream. I've wanted to shout, "You are embarrassing me!"

I mean when they commit five errors and get three hits against a team that has won only three games all year and the pitcher looks like he's never been near the mound before, I begin to believe I have failed the kids, parents, and perhaps, even my country. After all, if we have a superior team, how else could we lose? It must be the coaching . . . at least that's what I'm thinking. And that's what I'm thinking everyone else is thinking.

I imagine the parents are saying to themselves and each other, "This is awful. What are these guys teaching the kids at practice? Whose bright idea was it to have these guys coach in the first place? Jeeze, ***I*** could tell the kids to hit the cutoff man."

More than likely, though, everyone else is saying, "What a game. Wow. I can't believe we lost. The kids were really bad today. Oh well, they're 12 years old. Who is up for dinner?" The parents on my team, at least, are understanding and supportive. But that doesn't stop the irrational, insecure thoughts from popping to mind . . . especially in the middle of the night.

For the most part, I've resisted the urge to yell at the kids. It's not easy, though. They aren't putting forth the effort, the performance is lackluster, they are indifferent, the results are poor, and I feel it all reflects on my ability as a coach.

Ultimately it boils down to the simple fact that coaches can't want it more than the kids. They have to eventually rise to the occasion. As Sam likes to say, coaches coach and players play. My role is to keep trying new things while continuing to support them with suggestions, instruction, insight, and motivation.

It will cause psychological pain and physical discomfort to endure the slump, but that's a big part of our job as coach — to be that voice of reason and rock of support. Remaining positive is how I lead them out of the slump.

May 4

The Birth of a Baseball Koan

Note: *A koan is a statement or question that is unanswerable by rational thought and must be addressed by intuition. With roots in Zen Buddhism, a sage will often pose a koan to teach and test a student's ability to use insight. A couple of famous koans are, "Two hands clapping makes a sound. What is the sound of one hand clapping?" and "If a tree falls in the forest and there's nobody there to hear it, did it make a sound?"*

We couldn't seem to do anything right last night. We were enduring a 13 - 1 pounding, having made more than our share of blunders. Batters swung at bad pitches and watched others float through the zone for strike three. Pitchers had trouble throwing it near the plate, and when they did, the other team crushed the ball. Our fielders, perhaps distracted by the merry-go-round of base runners, committed five errors in the first three innings.

Early on it was clear we'd have to endure one of those nights where we simply didn't have it. The strategy is to learn as much as you can, get through it as quickly as possible, and then focus on the next game. Easier said than done . . . these are tough games on coaches.

In the top of the fourth they had runners on second and third with two outs and our pitcher, the fourth of the game, got the batter to hit a high popup in the infield. This would surely be the third out and allow us to bat in the bottom of the fourth. If we didn't score three runs, the game would, mercifully, be over.

As the ball topped out about 120 feet above the pitcher's mound, I heard nothing. No fielders were calling for the ball. In fact, none seemed to be moving to make the play. They all stood as if in quick-dry cement looking back and forth at each other and the ball. On the open seas you'd be hearing shouts from the crow's nest, "Iceberg! Iceberg!"

During re-entry the ball picked up speed and "splashed down" about equal distance from the pitching mound and first and second bases. Our nearest fielder was the second baseman.

Since there were two outs, their base runners were moving on the play. Our first baseman realized this, and on the third bounce of the ball, ran over, scooped it up and threw to the catcher . . . about a second late to tag out the sliding runner. Instead of being out of the inning, they scored two runs to enjoy a 15 - 1 lead and we still had only two outs.

Frustration propelling me into action, I took four quick steps out of the dugout and then stopped. What could I say to add value? I stood with hat in hand and jaw wide open. Staring at the blank expressions on the faces of my players, I was just as speechless as they were moments ago when the ball was in the air.

A voice in the back of my head was the only thing I heard. It screamed, "They're 12-years-old, for crying out loud! How many times have we told them to talk to each other? How many times have we told them to be aggressive and go for popups in the infield? Didn't we spend several minutes on this at practice last week? Do we really look that inept and poorly coached?"

It's times like this where the mounting aggravation morphs into sarcasm, and with the right amount of nurturing, can transform into existential humor. As I watched our pitcher kick the dirt off the rubber and begin to dig in against the next hitter I asked myself a question in the form of a baseball koan:

"If a batter hits a popup and no infielder calls for it, does the ball hitting the ground still make a sound?"

The small, aggravated voice in the back of my head replied, "It might but nobody can hear it over the smack of the coach's palm striking the middle of his forehead."

As Zen practitioners know, the answer to a koan comes through contemplative meditation, not Western reasoning or logic.

That's also true of our current losing streak.

May 5

The Unlikely Hero

I think the good old Yellow Jackets have pulled out of our slump. We beat the Bears last night 13 - 2 thanks to Jaime, an unlikely hero. Jaime has played baseball the last three years, but it has always been a filler sport for him. And, physically he hasn't grown much in the last year so he's smaller than most of the kids — this jump to AAA has been big for him.

So when he got a hit in our first tournament game last weekend I was happy for him, but I didn't think much of it. That, however, was the beginning of a hitting streak that may have awoken the entire team.

In the week span where we lost five games, Jaime had seven hits in seven at-bats and walked in four other plate appearances. He was the lone bright spot in this team slump and he amassed his hits quietly — because the coaches were focused on what was going wrong, we missed what was going right.

Last night as I talked to the kids before the game, I singled out Jaime and praised him for his seven-for-seven effort and said that he'd raised his batting average 85 points. The demeanor of the team immediately changed. They patted Jaime on the back, jokingly called him a show-off, and congratulated him for his performance. I think they realized that as a team they had wasted his effort.

I soon sensed an energy and enthusiasm from all 11 players I hadn't seen in a week. It was as if they simply decided to show up and play. After we scored six runs in the first inning the slump was a distant memory.

Thanks, Jaime! Your hard work accomplished what the coaching staff couldn't . . . the motivation to perform.

May 6

Parents

I've been extremely fortunate this season to have 10 sets of very supportive parents. Playing time, fairness, my approach to the game, instruction, or organization have not been issues. I've had questions here and there, and I've done things differently to accommodate a request or suggestion, but nothing has bubbled into a parental concern or problem.

My fortune is likely the result of three things: Good setup, good communication/relationship building, and good people.

First, I think we did a great job up front explaining our goals to prospective players and parents. **Fun, learn,** and **compete** resonated with many, but not all. Those who had other ideas went on to find a team that better aligned with their priorities. For those comfortable with this approach, we continued to reinforce a common definition of the terms and what that would mean on and off the field. Starting with clear expectations was essential.

Second, I see communication as my number one off-the-field responsibility as head coach. It's important on the field too, but building relationships with parents has been invaluable. Letting them get to know me, how I think and act, what my priorities are, how I interact with the kids, and how I teach begins to give them a comfort level with me as a coach and person. I go out of my way to talk to parents during down moments before games and at practice. I carry on email conversations with others throughout the week. Yes, it takes time — time I often don't feel I have. But if I don't invest the sweat to build these relationships, I'm going to spend five times the effort trying to patch, smooth, repair, and rebuild connections later on. If I have a good relationship with individuals, I'm much more likely to get told early on when something isn't going right or be granted the benefit of the doubt if things don't turn out as planned.

This role is similar to being a manager in the workplace. As a manager of people, I need to get to know everyone who works for me as a person. I need to know what their interests are, what's important to them, and what their hot buttons are. I need to treat each of them as an individual, not employee (or parent) number eight. Employees value different things — depending on the person and their life situation, money, time off, flexible schedule, challenging work, or a promotion could be their number on priority. A good manager will know those things about her team and try to get everyone what they need. Fair, but not necessarily equal or the same.

The same principle applies to a youth coach. Last week Brandon's grandmother was in town for a game and I gave him a little extra playing time at shortstop. I have also moved kids up in the batting order a spot or two for special non-baseball reasons. Another parent told me her son was struggling with his work habits in school, so I was able to help reinforce good routines on the field and relate them to his academics. I can't do everything for everyone, but knowing these things makes it easier for me to deliver on a lot of little things throughout the season. And, often, it's the little things that mean a lot.

Probably most importantly, though, our team has a great set of parents. They are good people. They care about their kids and they want the best for them. They're a very unselfish group, believing that the goal is for all of the kids to have fun and enjoy success. They understand and accept the fact that at times they may have to compromise. They appreciate that they are in this together. They support me, they support each other, and they support each other's kids.

Again, I'm fortunate. Very fortunate. Not everyone thinks this way. And it is rare to have 11 great families together on the same team.

The head coach of another team, Joe, confessed to me yesterday that he's having a few frustrating parent issues. While we were on the phone scheduling a scrimmage, Joe complained about several parents on his team who are deadbeats. They're those people who will do absolutely nothing to help, yet are willing to work exceptionally hard at getting out of simple obligations.

Early in the season he was having trouble getting parents to step forward to help with anything. They proudly pledged their support with the usual, "If there's anything I can do, let me know." Often it was accompanied by a smile, handshake, and a twinkle in the eye. But when the time came to help with uniform selection, hosting a team meeting, designing the team banner, creating a team Web site, or being the team accountant, things got very quiet.

Too quiet.

So, like the fabled little red hen, Joe did it himself. Later, he needed a team mom. He sent out several emails to the parents asking for a volunteer . . . nothing.

Joe's several phone calls netted a disappointing, "I'm pretty busy right now, let me think about it." Finally, in desperation, he sent out another email plea in the form of an "update." The email indicated that parents should visit a Web site to see the response so far for the team mom role (that site featured, simply, the sound of crickets chirping . . . the perfect symbol of all quiet . . . nothing happening!). That guilt eventually produced a team mom, who, surprisingly, already had a full-time job. The six stay-at-home moms on Joe's team said they didn't have a couple of hours every other week to coordinate and organize.

As I shook my head in disbelief at his story, I told Joe about my experience as an assistant coach three years ago. The head coach organized an end-of-the-season party for the 12 families on the team. With his own money Greg had pizza and soft drinks delivered. A group of six parents arrived with their kids and they asked him what time he thought the event would be over. In retrospect it seemed like a fair question. Greg said everyone could stay as long as the kids were having fun playing together, but probably an hour and a half. With that, the parents nodded their heads, turned around, and went out to dinner, leaving their three kids behind. Oh, yes, they did!

For the first time in our conversation I got Joe to laugh, albeit after a groan and a "No way!!" He had to admit that his situation wasn't that bad . . . not daycare bad!

This conversation with Joe led me to believe that if Jeff Foxworthy had been a youth baseball coach, (rather than hanging out with rednecks), he might have come up with a slightly different (and probably less lucrative) list to easily identify groups of people. Here's my take on how he'd describe deadbeat parents . . .

You might be a deadbeat parent if . . .

. . . you forget to slow down the car when you drop your kid off at practice.

. . . you schedule conference calls for the third inning stretch.

. . . you've never met the team mom.

. . . you have no idea how heavy the team's gear bag is.

. . . you had no idea there even was a team gear bag.

. . . you enjoy watching others chase foul balls during batting practice.

. . . you've told the team mom, "I gave at the office."

. . . you find the "uninterrupted quiet times" at games the most productive parts of your workday.

. . . you're miffed that the coach is five minutes late to pick up your kid and drive him to and from practice for the seventh time this month.

. . . you believe in the snack fairy . . . and are certain it is she who brings snacks and drinks to the kids after the game.

. . . you take pride in being the first car out of the parking lot after games.

. . . you have a better chance of knowing how many unread messages are on your Blackberry than knowing the score of the game.

. . . you enjoy watching others wade through the knee-deep weeds to find foul balls.

. . . generally speaking, you're able to reply to the coach's emails within 10 business days.

. . . you've spent 30 minutes, or more, racking your brain to come up with an excuse for not fulfilling a coach's request, which, by the way, would have taken only 15 minutes to complete in the first place.

... the team mom has hired a guy named Guido to talk to you about paying up on your fair share for last month's team BBQ.

... you believe *mandatory* does not apply to you.

Joe and I concluded that there's a key difference between parents and coaches. As a coach I bring a true passion to the baseball experience. Parents, though, bring expectations. Expectations about me, of me, about the team, of their kid, what they should receive, and how much effort this experience will be for them. Some are realistic and fair; some are not.

This means that even though they may at times share my passion, as a leader, I must always manage their expectations.

May 7

Sliding at Second – Part 3

Over the weekend Steve got ejected in the top of the first inning for running over the catcher on a play at the plate. Although he knew he had to slide, his dad told him that in the "old days" players could run over the catcher, like they do in the big leagues. Steve wasn't trying to hurt the other kid, he simply put his arms over his chest and ran him over. Unfortunately, it was an easy call for the umpire and Steve watched the rest of the game from the bleachers behind home plate. I felt bad for him having to sit things out, but with all the time we've spent on explaining the need to slide, he deserved it.

My initial thought was that this incident should be the final time we fail to slide at a base. With all of the explanation, instruction, me getting thrown out of a game, etc., you'd think there would be no way a player on the team could not understand what needed to be done — and do it!!

Sadly, it isn't that easy, at least for this coach. We played three games in this weekend tournament and I had four players, other than Steve, fail to slide when there was a close play. The disease is rapidly infecting the entire team. Geez, with the way they follow directions you'd think they were almost teenagers . . .

Several of the parents are starting to see the absurdity of the situation. They get an uncomfortable smile and shake their heads in disbelief, sharing my frustration while unsure of what to do with their kid to get the proper behavior.

I will spend time at practice this week again explaining the rule and my expectations and then we'll have each kid slide to a base 20 times . . . and, before every game I will remind them again.

Baseball can be a complex game. This is some of its appeal. But this whole sliding at a base thing is really, really pretty darn simple . . . I mean, really . . .

May 8

React Mode Warning Sign #3 – Rutted

After reflecting on the slump of last week, I think I was stuck in a rut of how to help the kids break out. Yeah, I tried a number of different approaches from reasoning to humor, reinforcing my expectations, and instruction. But they've heard all of those things from me before at different times. And often they work. But this time when they didn't, I kept trying the same things. I was stuck in a rut with my thinking and approach.

Being in a rut is another warning sign of a *Reaction.* I was locked in to the narrow slice of "knowing" what the solution must be and the "comfort" of having had success with that approach before. But I was missing the larger picture . . . what I was doing wasn't working and the kids needed something different. The situation had changed but my approach stayed the same. I suppose ruts are comforting. The outcome may not be ideal, but we at least know what to expect. Some people say the same is true of fast food . . .

Jaime gave me a way to break out of the rut and focus on something different. His success gave me a new motivational tool. It was there the whole time, but I was too focused on the narrow, wallowing in the disbelief that my tried and true solution wasn't working.

May 10

Be Humble

Note to self — the game of baseball is not as easy as you think it should be.

It can be a very humbling to get out on the field and play the game. Sometimes as coaches we forget that. For most of us it has been 20 or 30 years since we put on the uniform and crossed the lines in a competitive situation. That's why I enjoy playing in the adult baseball 35-and-over league.

In my game yesterday I was up to the plate early in the game with one out and runners on second and third. We were ahead by one run and needed a base hit to crack things open and get a comfortable lead. I was anxious and wanted to be the guy to make it happen (I've told my players they should ***want*** to be in this situation).

I knew that the pitcher was going to start me off with a slider or a breaking ball. I had watched him do that to the previous three hitters. He went from a full windup and I saw the ball immediately on his release . . . I was right! He threw me a weak curveball! I could see the spin as it left his hand. In the small fraction of a second it took for the ball to get half way to the plate I had calculated that it was going to break low and away, out of the strike zone.

"Don't swing!!" yelled the voice in the back of my head. It was a bad pitch that I wouldn't be able to hit hard. But, like so many of my players, I was anxious. I really, really wanted to swing. I had guessed right on the pitch. I knew where the ball was going. I desperately wanted to drive in the two runs.

So did I listen to my own sage advice or get swept away in the excitement of the moment?

Of course I swung at it. It was just below my knees about three inches outside of the plate when my bat made contact. Eager, I reached out, swung too soon, and popped it up to the third baseman for an easy out.

So how many times have I told my players to be aware of what's going on, to know what the situation is, know what to do and have the discipline to do it? I expect them to do it. And here I am the coach and a player who has been in the game for almost 35 years and I still make the mistake. Dang!

Fortunately none of my players were there to see me do it . . . note to self: be humble.

What did I learn? ***Coaches would be surprised, and at times disgusted, at the mistakes they would make if they took the field for a 30-game season.*** My new mantra:

1. ***Instruct*** the kids to do it right.
2. ***Reinforce*** it at every opportunity.
3. ***Expect*** them to perform.
4. ***Understand*** when they fail.

The first three are pretty standard guidelines for coaches. I've added the fourth. Because I'm still playing the game myself, I'm reminded every time I lace up the cleats and take the field myself to respect how difficult it is to play the game well . . . consistently.

May 14

The Making of Tylerville

I remember using that time-honored parental phrase, "How do you know you won't like it until you try it?" with Alan. It was many years ago and I'm sure it involved some sort of green vegetable.

I used it again a few weeks ago with Tyler at practice when discussing the possibility of him playing centerfield. A short, fast lefty, outfield is a natural spot for him, but as a 12-year-old he's been looking at the outfield from the wrong perspective.

I explained to him, that, yes, when he was six or seven, his coaches may have at times tried to "hide" the weaker players in the outfield, hoping that the ball wouldn't be hit out there. I reminded him, though, that he was now 12 and there are a lot of balls hit to the outfield. A key to our success, I continued, was that pitchers would be able to count on the outfielders to catch the ball — if they couldn't, we were in big trouble as a team.

So we worked a few fundamentals with him, like how to take a good angle to get to the ball, how to have his momentum moving in when he caught it, and how to throw to the cutoff man. He picked it up pretty quickly but was still skeptical about "having" to play outfield.

Over the weekend though, that all changed. We officially designated centerfield as "Tylerville."

In one inning he made all three outs — the first two were fairly routine fly balls he caught easily. On the last one he made a sliding catch while charging hard on a ball that was dropping just over the infield. We all imagined the ESPN Sports Center highlight music, "Dun dun dunt. Dun dun dunt" as he held up his glove to show the umpire he'd made the play. Tyler sprinted in to the dugout all smiles, getting all sorts of high fives and pats on the head from his teammates.

Coach Sam said to the team, "From now on fly balls to centerfield will die in Tylerville."

After the game Tyler pulled me aside and said he was now happy to play centerfield, and, if it were okay with me, he'd like to start there in the second game of our doubleheader. He also asked if I would hit him a few more fly balls so he could practice.

Wow! It's amazing what a little encouragement, instruction, and positive reinforcement can do for a 12-year-old!

This is the icing on the cake for him — he's having a great season. He started in a horrible slump, not getting a hit in his first six games. He was almost tip-toeing to the plate, his head down, feet a bit pigeon-toed and the pensive, "I hope nothing bad happens this time" look on his worried face showed anything but confidence.

We kept encouraging him though, realizing that his struggles were more mental than anything mechanical in his swing. He was trying very hard to make a good impression on the coaches and his teammates. Like the other 10 players, he didn't want to be the weakest link on a team. He's also a kid that thinks a lot and can quickly get wrapped up in a spiral of despair.

Our approach with Tyler was to remain positive and not pressure him to get hits. We asked him to focus on having good at-bats, which meant taking a good swing at a good pitch. The results would then start to take care of themselves. At times we'd make minor adjustments to his mechanics, which were, more than anything else, a distraction to get him thinking about something other than his past performance. It helped to have him focus on doing something new with his swing and tune in to the possibility of success that could bring. Finally, I modified a line from my favorite baseball movie, *Bull Durham*, "Tyler, don't think — just see the ball and hit it."

In his last hitless game he had two good at-bats, a sharp ground out to shortstop and a fly ball to centerfield. He started to feel better about his chances of success and brought more confidence to the next game. That day he had three solid singles and stole two bases. This ignited a hot streak where he had 18 hits in 24 at-bats — a .750 clip!!

He's now all smiles, a confident player who can better handle his failures and has learned to stop thinking when it gets in his way of performing (although he'll often need help from his coaches to recognize that).

His dad told me during his hot streak that he really appreciated the coaching staff's strategy with Tyler and not putting pressure on him. His dad felt that the coaches showing patience and confidence in him rebuilt Tyler's self-confidence.

If we had yelled or pressured he might have imploded and had a horrible season, which would have killed his passion for the game. He could have been a casualty . . . a statistic . . . one of the 80 percent who quits by age 15.

Tyler's abrupt turnaround and the making of Tylerville are successes I'm very proud of this season. He had all of the skills and talent to succeed, we just indentified what was getting in the way, showed him how to overcome the obstacle, and gave him the opportunity to perform. Successes like this make all of the time and effort to be a coach worthwhile!

May 16

Learn Many Positions

Alan complained to me the other night that for the last few games I had been "sticking" him in the outfield for an inning or two. I bit my lip and let him vent a little as he laid out his case for why he shouldn't "have" to play there. He said it was boring and that he wasn't any good in the outfield. He finished his rant saying, "I'd rather sit the bench than play outfield."

I decided to handle this one gently.

"I agree, Alan," I began. "I'm much happier and comfortable in the infield myself. The game moves at a different pace and I feel like I'm closer to the action."

Alan began to smile, believing he'd won the argument and that he now possessed a season ticket to play the infield.

"But you know how important the outfield is, right?" I asked.

"Yeah, Dad," he conceded.

"I mean when you are pitching, you want to have a good outfield to back you up, right?" I continued.

"Well, yeah," he said, this time a bit more hesitant, unsure of where my line of questioning was heading.

"So we agree it's an important position, you just don't like playing it, right?" I inquired.

“Yeah, I just don’t like playing out there,” he said.

Knowing the answer, I asked, “You’d rather play third base?”

“Yeah.”

“Okay. I get that. But follow me here for a minute,” I requested. “What happens in a few years when you get to high school and as a ninth grader you’re hitting really well, like you are now, and the junior varsity coach says he’d like to have your bat in his lineup?”

Alan hesitated. “I don’t know what you mean,” he said, obviously not familiar with the high school terms.

“Okay, you are a ninth grader — a freshman — playing on the freshman team with the other kids in your grade,” I explained.

“Yeah, I get that,” he said.

“Let’s say you’re hitting the cover off the ball and the junior varsity coach — junior varsity is for 11th graders — thinks you are ready to come play with kids two years older.”

Alan didn’t have to think about that, “That would be cool!” he exclaimed.

“Yes it would.” I smiled. “But what if there was a catch? What if you had to play left field to do that? What if the guy playing third base was a sophomore and hitting as well as you are? The coach wouldn’t bench him, he would look for a weaker link in his lineup and put you in there.”

Alan pondered the situation.

I continued, “The coach would look at the batting averages on his team and put you in for the left fielder who was hitting .119. Would you play left field then?”

“Of course,” said Alan, picturing himself playing with kids who were two years older.

"But what if you had never played left field?" I asked, bursting his bubble. "You'd be a weak link. You'd be letting down the pitcher and rest of the team if you didn't at least know how to play the position."

Alan saw my point.

"But if you were able to tell the coach that you had played outfield and were willing to work at it, he'd give you a shot, don't you think?" I questioned.

"Yeah, probably," he admitted.

"That's why I want you to learn several positions," I clarified. "Now is the time to do that — not in high school. It doesn't mean you won't get to play third base this year. It doesn't mean you can't prefer to play somewhere else. It just means you need to learn as many positions as possible and have the skills to be versatile."

Alan started to get it.

"That's how I got to be a pitcher in high school," I explained, looking for a way to cement the deal. "All I wanted was to play first base as a sophomore on junior varsity. One day the starting pitcher was sick and the coach asked who could pitch. I'd done it when I was younger so I volunteered. I ended up throwing a great game and became a pitcher for the rest of the season."

Alan nodded.

"The same thing happened my junior year," I continued. "I didn't want to pitch — I had decided first base was my spot. But early in the season we were playing the best team in our league, losing 7 - 0 in the third inning. The coach didn't want to waste any other pitchers so he put me in. I shut them out for four innings and we lost only 7 - 4. Because I did well the coach had me start a game the following week. I pitched a complete game and gave up only one run. The following Monday when the high school statistics were published in the newspaper, I was second in the state in earned run average — it was early in the season, but quite a thrill. None of that was part of my plan, but given the opportunity I decided that maybe I would give pitching a try. That's how I became a pitcher — not because it's what I wanted."

Alan didn't know quite what to say, so I tried to simplify the point.

"Look, buddy, you never know where you're going to end up or what opportunities the situation will present you with," I explained. "My advice is to learn as much as you can, be flexible, and show a willingness to give many different things a try."

Alan nodded and agreed that he'd give it another shot.

I think Alan now understands I'm not sticking him in the outfield as punishment. I'm simply trying to help him learn the game from a different perspective. Each position has its unique nuances and way of approaching the game. We can learn those only by doing.

My experience is that coaches and parents tend to get too caught up in locking kids down to one position too quickly. That will happen soon enough in high school. I think kids should play multiple sports, and similarly they should play multiple positions. If for no other reason, we simply don't know what a 10-year-old will look like when he's 15 or 18. Today's stud pitcher may have a below average arm by the time he's 16. If all he knows is pitching, he may be done.

But we shouldn't focus narrowly on preparing our kids for the high school game. Statistics show that only a handful will play varsity baseball in high school. Youth sports should be about learning and trying many different things — we have a great opportunity to ignite the passion for understanding the complexities of the game and each position on the field reveals another layer. Our job is to expand their horizons and stretch their imaginations, not limit their opportunities.

May 18

Memory Lane — A Mumford Electric Reunion

Last night we reassembled the coaching staff of Mumford Electric — the baseball team my dad coached when I was 11, 12 and 13 years old. Coaches Phil, Jim, and Carl, now in their late 60s, and Gary, Ben and I, the three sons, enjoyed the opportunity to reconnect and laugh about old times. Our three sons, now 12, 13 and 14 years old, listened to it all, getting, I'm sure, a very different picture of their dads and grandpas. And, the moms and wives spoke up frequently to ensure that the boys got the real story of what happened long ago.

It was an evening full of smiles and warm memories. Baseball was responsible for it all. The friendships were built around a mutual love of the game, and, although they laid dormant for 25 years, were powerful enough to quickly reconnect two generations and integrate a third. Baseball provided the language to bridge the gaps.

Jim, Carl, and Phil spoke with warmth about those three fantastic seasons. Their stories conveyed affection and passion for the game and that time in their lives. Coaching their sons and coaching together brought happiness, satisfaction, and meaning to that era.

However, Ben, Gary, and I were quick to chime in with our version of the facts. We amused ourselves remembering Gary's lack of speed, Ben's many short experiments with pitching, and my calamities on the base paths. We talked about the losses we should have won and the wins we should have lost. We laughed at the errors, marveled at the great plays, and questioned each other of the whereabouts of teammates long forgotten.

Later Gary, Ben, and I shared our recent coaching experiences — interestingly, all three of us ended up coaching our sons. As my mom listened to the three of us middle-aged kids talk, she noted that this conversation was the same as the ones that our dads had 25 years ago . . . the trials and tribulations with parents, umpires, other coaches, and kids never seem to change . . . only the names of those involved are different. We're just tenants . . . we seem to own the game for a while, but then pass it along to the next group coming through. I could see forward and backwards in the lines of history in my family room last night . . . and after the second round of beers, we began to re-write some of it too!

In our three hours together it's interesting that the topic of winning almost never came up. We did talk about the outcome of individual games, but none of us reflected on how many games we won or lost. Conversation was about funny things that happened, teammates, and things we learned.

Coaches and parents today get so wrapped up in winning. It struck me that it doesn't have to be that way. In my living room there were three competitive coaches with three competitive former youth baseball players. The three of us "kids" excelled in high school ball and all went on to play in college. Our focus last night wasn't on winning or losing . . . it was about the game, the richness it has brought to each of our lives, and the connections it has created with friends and family. So where is time and effort better spent? Developing a winning program and defeating all opponents at any cost, or providing the learning environment to have fun and create memories that last a lifetime?

Last night was a blast. I also have a much greater appreciation for what our dads went through. I think they got a sense of closure that brought peace and a sense of accomplishment, especially as they looked at us standing next to our kids. They felt they'd done their duty and had passed a passion for the game on to the next generation . . . and that the three of us were fulfilling our obligation to instill it in the next one.

I went to bed last night with a warm feeling. I rekindled several old friendships, shared some great laughs, and remembered many good times. Perhaps most importantly, I left with the conviction that I'm doing things right for Alan. Coaching is an important role in society while bringing meaning to everyone involved. And while I'm certainly making my share of mistakes (which Alan and his buddies will point out 25 years from now), I'm proud to be making a difference. It's a thrill to see it come full circle.

I suppose when we gather in Alan's family room 25 years from now, it likely won't be much different than last night . . . except Alan will buy the beer.

May 21

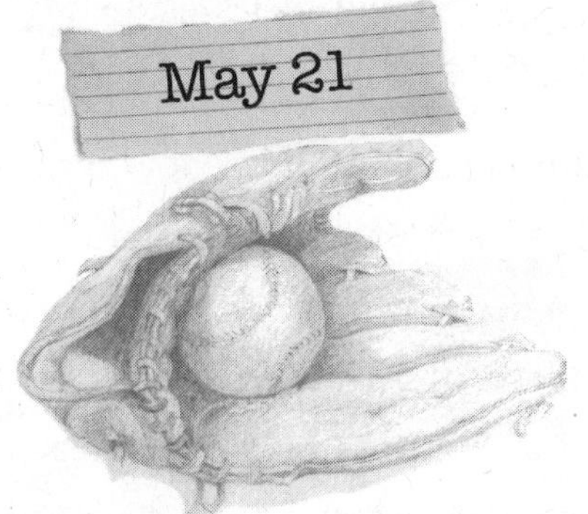

The Buffaloes Incident

I have to vent after last night's game. It's amazing to me how some of the biggest jerks can end up coaching kids. These ego-driven guys are obvious a mile away . . . everything they do is for them or about them, not the development or enjoyment of the kids. Even more perplexing and troubling is that parents let their kids play for these misguided idiots.

Last night, two of these characters showed that youth sports turns ugly when the wrong people are involved. After a good close game where they pulled out a dramatic win in the last inning, the opposing coaches confronted Sam and me in the middle of the field and wanted to fight . . . and this was a game they won!

I don't mind losing to another team that's playing well, hustling, and displays good sportsmanship. Most of the teams we play are filled with good people. The parents, kids, and coaches are the type I'd like to believe my team would enjoy going out for pizza with after the game. However, after last night I'm sure I couldn't stand to be in the same room with these coaches.

Leading the Buffaloes were two guys who spent the entire two-hour game with disgusted looks on their faces. They used extreme profanity and personal insults to motivate their team. They yelled incessantly at their players, calling them "stupid," "horrible" and "ridiculous." In between innings, and just out of earshot of the umpires, both would drop "F-bombs" to describe the play, situation, and even our players. Several of our parents overheard one coach say to his 12-year-olds, "You're not going to let those (expletive) beat you, are you?" as he pointed to our dugout. In between these fits of rage he and his assistant sat in the dugout with looks of complete contempt for their team. Clearly nobody on that side of the field was having fun.

We gave the game away, letting them score five runs in the top of the sixth inning to take a lead. In that wild inning, our pitcher hit a batter in the leg. As I would discover later, the other coach was convinced that we did it on purpose. There had been no other hit batters, no confrontations, no hard slides or anything else that would provoke either team into such behavior. The other coach spoke to the umpire briefly as his player hobbled down to first base, but he quickly returned to his first base coaching box. As I look back on it, he likely lost the gusto to push the issue because he realized that the hit batter happened to be the tying run and he was now on first base.

From a strategic perspective, this certainly was not the situation to purposely hit someone. No big league manager would put the tying run on base like that. And, more importantly, from a youth sports perspective, there is NEVER a time to intentionally throw at another kid. I've told my pitchers they can throw inside to keep a batter from leaning over the plate, but I'd never instruct or condone a pitcher intentionally throwing at another kid.

After the game as the teams trotted across the field and shook hands, the other coach grabbed my forearm, held on and pulled me closer to him and said, "I have a real problem with your team and the lack of sportsmanship you guys display."

I was taken aback, still ringing from a blown four-run lead. I quickly replayed the game in my mind but couldn't remember any incident that gave his comment any context. I couldn't believe these wretched role models who yelled profanity all game were confronting me about anything having to do with sportsmanship.

I replied, "What do you mean, coach?" and pulled my arm away from him. I was honestly looking for an answer. If we had done something unsportsmanlike I wanted to know about it.

He glared at me and seethed, "You threw at our batter and your shortstop laughed and told the pitcher to do it again."

I had heard nothing like that from our players and couldn't imagine either of our shortstops saying anything remotely like that. Both were great kids and good sports.

He continued with eyes bulging, "You need to call your players out and stop this."

My mind was racing, still trying to figure out where this confrontation was coming from. It hadn't registered yet that they only wanted confrontation — I was still problem-solving.

I replied, "Look coach, we did not throw at your hitter. It was the tying run, why would we do that? I wouldn't have my kids throw at anybody. I would like to know what was said and, if you know, who said it. Then I will handle it. The discipline of my team is my responsibility."

I was starting to get angry. Any reasonable coach would have been less confrontational with me if they genuinely thought there was an issue. And, more importantly, they would have helped me problem-solve by providing specifics about what they heard or saw.

This guy's actions, though, clearly indicated he was looking for a fight, not help me improve the behavior of my team. He grabbed my arm again and pulled me even closer than before. He stepped up on his toes, puffed his chest into mine, and thrust his face close enough that I could smell the pinch of tobacco nestled between his cheek and gum. "You need to call your team out, coach. You need to take care of this," he growled with a crazed-animal look in his eyes. I was in college the last time I was that close to someone who clearly just wanted to fight.

I had a decision to make. It was an easy one. If I stayed on the field much longer, one way or another, the situation was going to degenerate fast. Any further interaction with these two guys was going to escalate and they were both doing their best to provoke an incident. I could be right, or I could be effective. I could *React* to the adrenaline, ego and frustration, or *Respond* as a positive role model and reinforce to everyone watching what youth sports should be about.

I forcefully pulled away from him. I kept eye-contact and declared, "Like I said, coach, the discipline of my team is my responsibility." I took a step towards my dugout without breaking eye contact, pointed my finger at him and said, "If you can let me know what was said and who said it, I'm all ears. Otherwise, we're done." I didn't wait for a reply and strode towards my dugout.

He started to follow me, yelling something about sportsmanship. Our parents were terrific. They began booing the other coach and one yelled, "Come on coach, way to set an example for your kids."

Their support shamed the other coach enough that he stopped, alone in the middle of the field. After a few more suggestions from our parents for better behavior, he turned and walked back to his dugout.

I was really angry, having just lost a four-run lead in the last inning and then been inches away from a fight. Shaking with adrenalin, I stormed into our dugout and started packing my gear.

I felt proud — teetering on the brink of a brawl that would make a top-10 list of lowlights in youth sports, I made a good choice. I was equally pleased that our group of kids and parents was unified in our willingness to not accept the other team's behavior, yet dignified in our *Response* by not resorting to profanity or violence. After all, 22 kids were in the dugouts packing their gear and watching things unfold.

Again I come back to the two points. First, how do idiots like that get to be coaches in the first place? Second, how can parents watch something like that and allow their kids to continue to play for them?

I mean, who are these guys? They were probably below-average high school players back in their heydays. Over the years their ability has declined with their advancing age but their perception of past glory has grown exponentially. It is obvious to anyone who has played the game that the way these guys compete and handle themselves, they are not "has beens" . . . they are "never weres." They are now living a self-indulgent myth of past greatness that they sell parents while recruiting and use to impress and intimidate kids.

Guys like this give youth sports a bad name and make it difficult for everybody else to have fun and enjoy the game. It makes it tough to teach the kids the game of baseball in that ugly, confrontational, and hostile environment.

I mean, who are they out there for? Are they focused on the kids or are they feeding their egos, trying to re-live a past they never had? I think they're just unhappy people. They're unhappy at work and unhappy at home, looking for a place to take out the frustration and aggression. Unfortunately all the conditions are right on the youth sports field . . .

Everyone in the league has a responsibility to root this out.

All of us.

Parents need to confront their coaches when they cross the line. They need to report coaches like this to the league by providing as many details as possible — in writing. Coaches need to police each other. Umpires need to remind coaches and parents that we're out there for the kids. Leagues need to crack down and randomly observe coaches who are suspect or have been reported. Doing nothing allows the behavior to continue. Rationalizing that someone else will take care of it silently condones the actions.

We all have responsibility.

It takes a whole community to create a positive baseball experience for our youth.

May 22

React Mode Warning Sign #4 – Cranial Bypass

I am so glad I didn't act on the first thing that came to mind the other night after the game when the coach of the Buffaloes got in my face. Obviously he wanted a confrontation. My initial thought was to push back and not let him bully me. This original idea was based on my ego not wanting to look weak, anger at being called a poor sport, and frustration with blowing a four-run lead in the last inning. I was in no frame of mind to be pushed around verbally or physically. I'll admit the first thing that came to mind was to forcefully remove his hands from my arm and yell some choice words back in his face. I'm thankful, though, that in that split second I had to make a decision I didn't act on those thoughts and emotions.

Fortunately I was in problem-solving mode, trying to figure out why he was complaining about our sportsmanship. Because I continued searching for an answer, I bought myself a little time to think the situation through and saw a non-violent way to walk from the altercation. I was frustrated and angry, but I didn't let those emotions dictate my actions. I was able, amid the adrenalin and testosterone, to remember what was most important in that particular situation: being a positive role model and creating a safe learning environment where the kids could have fun.

Often, however, we do act on the first thing that pops into mind. We don't consider the consequences or try to integrate our longer-term goals. This fast action on the first option we see should be called cranial bypass. Suggested words or actions can come from anywhere — thoughts, emotions, something we heard, watching others doing it, or just the ether. When we rashly act on these, we're circumventing the other important parts of the brain that weigh consequences or pose new options. The idea isn't filtered, aligned, or considered — just acted upon. Later we often hear ourselves say, "I don't know why I did that . . . I just didn't think . . ."

I sometimes catch myself doing this in games. The shortstop makes a bad throw to first which allows the runner to get to second base on the overthrow. I holler, "Make a good throw!"

Well, duh! Thanks, Captain Obvious.

That was the first thing that came to mind. Yes, it is what we need the shortstop to do . . . but he already knows that. It's not like my insight is a news flash to him.

"Gee, thanks, coach for pointing that out. For the last five years I thought I was trying to throw it past the first baseman. Thanks for setting me straight . . ."

I've not helped him figure out what he did wrong, only announced to the world that he made a mistake on something that appears to be very simple. Did that help him achieve **fun, learn, compete**? No, no, and no.

I'm better off biting my tongue and thinking about why he made the mistake. Were his feet in good position? Did he field the ball cleanly? Did he stay down through the throw? Where was his release point —

did he throw sidearm? I need to help him diagnose the problem and offer constructive feedback and further instruction, not fulfill the immediate desire to tell him he messed up.

But that can be tough to do . . . that first thing that comes to mind can seem like the obvious thing to say. It can become a habit . . . thought comes to me, I open mouth, words come out . . . wait, what did I just say?

I'm glad I was able to avoid this type of cranial bypass the other night with the Buffaloes. That would have been a *Reaction* I'd have to pay for all season, and perhaps beyond.

May 24

Sliding at Second – Part 4

So now I know why coaches (and parents) get gray hair. This whole sliding at bases issue is going to push me over the edge. In the last game Bobby stole second and didn't slide although it was a close play. I was in the third base coach's box and turned to the kids in the dugout behind me and said, "Guys, what do we do at second base?"

They were silent for a minute and then realized what Bobby hadn't done. After some hesitation and nervous glances a couple of them, not in unison, said "Slide, coach?"

I nodded my head and asked it again of the whole bench, this time louder, "What do we do when we get to a base?"

This time they got it and said, "Slide, Coach!" in unison and rather loudly.

I felt we had finally mastered this one . . .

Two innings later Alan stole second and didn't slide, again just barely beating a good throw from the catcher. I stood silently in disbelief. I stared at him with hat in hand, both arms quizzically out from my side, unable to form words. After a few seconds of him staring back at me I said simply, "Alan, you HAVE to slide."

Exasperated, I turned to the bench and asked, more for my own sanity than anything, "Guys, what do we do at second base?"

A loud chorus of, "Slide coach!" rebounded back to me.

Okay they did hear me last time. Check. I wasn't talking to myself. Check. I wasn't hearing things. Check. I'm not going crazy . . . the jury is still out on that one.

Probing a bit further I said to the dugout, "Guys, **WHY** do we slide at second base?"

I got some good answers.

"To avoid the tag."

"To slow down so we don't overrun the base."

"Because you told us to."

"It's the rule?"

Great, I thought, maybe they have been listening. The umpire interrupted play and sauntered out from behind the catcher. He slowly pulled out his brush and bent over to dust off the plate.

"So guys," I continued. My two-month-long exasperation with this really, really simple baseball fundamental was spilling over into a sarcastic line of reasoning. I thought humor would provide a way to vent the building frustration I felt. "They put this stuff down in the infield around the bases, what is it? It's brown . . ."

I got a few puzzled looks from the kids. Finally Brandon said, "Um, dirt, coach?"

"Yes!" I shouted with a smile and enthusiasm. "Right! And why would they put the dirt there?"

The players were huddled in the far end of the dugout near where I was standing, separated from me only by the chain-link fence. They were brimming with enthusiasm and, surprisingly, starting to enjoy this!

One of the great things about kids, especially 12-year-olds, is that their senses of humor are becoming more sophisticated as they transform into young men. Tapping into that is a good strategy — I can sometimes make a point using humor without having to hit them over the head with the lesson I'm trying to teach.

The kids' wit was starting to match mine and they began reeling off answers, demonstrating that they did know what to do at second base and why.

"They put the dirt there to make it smooth?"

"To make it soft?"

"So we don't get hurt?"

"So we can slide?"

"So we can get dirty!" shouted Tyler, now really getting excited.

"Yes," I said, to the last answer, "but if, and ONLY IF, you slide, right?"

"Right coach, only if you slide," said a proud Tyler, smiling and shaking his head while giving a cocky look to his teammates.

The umpire had not yet set play on the field so I continued with the kids. "So they put this soft stuff called dirt down around the bases so that we will slide, right?"

"Right coach!" yelled eight enthusiastic players.

"And that's why they don't cover the infield in, say, concrete right?"

They agreed without hesitation. "Right coach, no concrete."

I thought it best to leave them with a question to ponder. "So what else don't they put in the infield that would prevent you from sliding?"

It took them a few seconds to think through the complexity of the question.

"Broken glass?" offered Tommy.

"Right! Broken glass!" I exclaimed. "They wouldn't put broken glass in the infield. Who would slide on that? What else?"

The creative juices were spilling over, each trying to be a bigger wise guy than the last.

"Rocks and boulders, coach!" yelled Zach with a grin on his face.

"Furniture," Reed said.

I smiled at them and backpedaled a few steps towards the coaching box. Play was about to resume, and I had made my point. I turned my attention to Alan at second base and heard a few more good ones.

"Asphalt," Tyler shouted.

"Nails; big sharp rusty ones," said Brandon, really pondering the pain they might cause.

"Rakes and shovels," said another.

I almost inhaled a sunflower seed when Bobby said, "Chainsaws."

I think we may have it now. I can't believe it took three months to get this, but I'll take the victory!

May 25

Passing the Torch

The Mumford Electric coaching staff reunion the other night got me thinking about the importance of passing the torch to the next generation of baseball coaches. Seeing the three families and the three generations of ballplayers and coaches made me appreciate how fortunate I have been to grow up in a baseball family. I owe my parents, sister Laurie, and grandparents an awful lot for the experiences I've had. They all sacrificed so I could enjoy the game. The repayment of this debt, though, should be an enduring thanks and vigorous effort to pay it forward. That's how it has worked in my family.

Long ago Grandpa passed his love for the game to Dad, who handed it to me, and now I'm giving it to Alan. But how, exactly, does this happen? Where does this love, or passion for the game come from? I think there are two major sources. First is on the field playing the game, experiencing the strategy, complexity, challenge, and fun it has to offer. Ken Burns more than did this justice in his fantastic documentary.

Baseball passion, though, has a second source. We get it from the people around us. The experiences we share with one another while watching or talking about baseball nurture our passion. And, who better than family to provide fuel for the fire?

My grandpa loved baseball but had to stop playing when he was in eighth grade. It was the 1920s and he quit school to get a job and help support his family. But his passion for the game smoldered until he had a family of his own, and then, throughout the years, coached his three sons. He had a wealth of coaching stories, some of them probably true, that taught me about baseball in the "olden days."

One I heard many times was how he named my uncle's team.

At the league meeting they went around the room and asked each coach the name of his team. I hadn't really thought about it until it was my turn. My mind went blank and the only thing I could think of was the name of our sponsor. So instead of being the Athletics, Red Sox, or Browns, we were the Jasso Builders.

Thus, I understand, he started a trend in Sugar Creek, Missouri of naming teams after their sponsors. Grandpa also showed me how he threw a sidearm, or "roundhouse" curveball. I was fascinated with the tale of Ironhead, the "not-so-bright" catcher, who hit a homerun in the bottom of the last inning to win a game in which my uncle and the opposing pitcher both had no-hitters. Grandpa was also convinced that all you had to do was watch a batter's feet to see if they were going to be a good hitter. When we'd watch the Saturday game of the week on TV, he'd repeat throughout the game, "Did you see his feet? Just watch his feet on the next pitch."

Dad, too, had his stories. I always enjoyed hearing him recall when he was playing against his friend Herbie. Dad was trying to steal second base and his friend came over to take the throw. At the last second Dad yelled, "Look out Herbie!" The boy jumped out of the way, missing the ball and Dad slid in safe. I'm not sure Herbie was still his friend after the game, but that's another story.

My favorite tale, though, was the time when Dad rounded third base too far. His coach was the animated sort, and in the process of hollering at Dad to get back to the bag, he swallowed an entire mouthful of tobacco. I loved hearing Dad describe that his coach's face turned several shades of red and how, for the rest of the game, the guy was unable to talk — only cough, sputter, and spit.

As I look back on my childhood, some of my best times were listening to Kansas City Royals games on the radio with Dad. Growing up in Denver in the 1970s, we didn't have a major league team, and since our family was from Kansas City and it was the closest major league town, we religiously followed the Royals.

Somehow Dad found a radio station, KRVN's 50,000 watts in Lexington, Nebraska, that carried the Royals games. We could only get the station at night, apparently after they boosted their power. Because we were 400 miles away from the transmitter, the signal would fade in and out and we'd momentarily lose the voices of Denny Matthews and Fred White calling the game. (What an impact this broadcasting duo had . . . I can remember their names 30 years later!)

We would listen and talk about the game, statistics, situations, and players. This is when Dad taught me to calculate batting and earned run averages and what "games back" in the standings meant. The absolute best was in August and September 1980 using my dad's new calculator to figure George Brett's batting average as he chased the magical plateau of .400. Calculators were rare and expensive back then (and large!), so getting to use one was a treat and I'd update my detailed records of Brett's hits and at-bats by looking at the daily box scores in the paper.

Dad and I would often be playing a game of cribbage while listening. Other times we'd be doing our own things — a high school math teacher, he'd be grading papers and I'd be sorting my baseball cards. It didn't really matter what we were doing — we were together, sharing a love for the game.

Now I'm in that position of responsibility of creating baseball passion and memories for my son. I've thought about the things I imagine Alan will remember. He loves playing in the weekend tournaments because they compact a lot of baseball into parts of two days while providing a lot of down time in between games where the kids can have fun goofing around together. He talks about eating out after games and playing the video games in the restaurant lobby. He also enjoys the sleepovers with teammates.

And, as we drive to and from practices and games, Alan asks me a lot of questions about when I played. He loves the stories, in part I suppose, because they take him to a far away place and enable him to know me at a different age at a different time. And, just like I pestered my dad to tell me about Herbie for the 40th time, Alan relentlessly asks me about my first homerun, when I started pitching, and for other details of events and teammates I've long forgotten.

On the surface, it seems, I'm simply answering questions. I'm starting to realize, though, that I'm actually sharing the next batch of stories, something akin to an oral tradition where meaningful experiences are handed down from one generation to the next. They are, I believe, part of the bandwidth upon which we transfer our love for the game.

To confirm that I was on the right track, I asked Alan what he thought he would remember when he's my age.

"You mean 30 YEARS from now?" he asked, only to jab at my age.

I gave him a crusty "whatever" look and redirected. "What will you be telling your kids about baseball when you were growing up?"

He thought for only a moment and replied, "You getting tossed."

Great.

All the effort I've put in this year to give him and the rest of the team the best possible baseball experience and my lowlight is his highlight? One small moment of indiscretion on my part becomes his most vivid and lasting youth sports memory?

"I don't think your kids will believe you," I said. "At that point you'll be the dad and I'll be sweet old gray-haired Grampy. They won't think I'm capable of such behavior."

Alan paused. Then showing a remarkable natural sense of timing that debaters and comedians would kill for, revealed his ace in the hole.

"Mom will sell you out," he grinned.

Dang! I thought to myself, "Nicely played," not wanting to admit defeat aloud.

As I reflect upon this tradition of transferring the passion between generations, I'm only now able to fully appreciate how much Dad gave while I was growing up . . . and how much Grandpa gave when Dad was young. It wasn't until I had a family, job, and life of my own that I realized the breadth and depth of his contribution. As parent coaches we lay down many sacrifice bunts to move our kids along the game's base paths.

Thanks, Grandpa. Thanks, Dad.

I hope Alan says the same thing 30 YEARS from now . . .

It's not just the dads that sacrifice. Mom, my sister Laurie, and both grandmas gave huge amounts of time to cheer at my games in lieu of other activities. Beyond that, they cooked meals, washed uniforms, patched skinned knees, comforted bruised egos, and offered unconditional support. Clearly it takes everyone pulling together to create a great youth baseball experience.

Thanks, Mom. Thanks, Laurie. Thanks, Grandma Marion. Thanks, Grandma Ursula.

May 27

Seeing the Fruits of Your Labor

Yesterday after school Alan and his friend Quinn were shooting baskets in the driveway and I realized as a coach you don't always get to see the fruits of your labors. I was an assistant basketball coach for Alan and Quinn for five seasons until they were 10 years old. Quinn has a lot of athletic talent, but often struggles with the fundamentals — he invents his own way of doing things that sometimes work but turn a coach's hair prematurely gray.

The perfect example was Quinn would always drive in for a layup and scoop the ball from his hip, rather than use his height as an advantage and shoot the ball from above his head. I worked tirelessly in practice to get him to shoot it correctly, explaining that it was easier, more accurate, and less likely to get blocked. In games I'd go sit by him on the bench and compliment him for driving to the basket ... but emphasize that he had the shot blocked by a kid six inches shorter because he was releasing the ball at his hip. Quinn, drenched in sweat and disappointed because he didn't score, would nod his head in understanding . . . and then go do the same darn thing.

For five seasons I worked on this. In the fifth season it became my pet project. He worked hard and I was relentless in calling his attention to what he'd just done — right or wrong I wanted him aware.

Finally in the last game of the season he did it right. He jumped with the correct foot, used his body to shield the ball from the defender, and released it above his head at the top of his jump. The ball gently bounced off the backboard and through the net. Two points!

At the team party after the game I was almost in tears describing the sense of accomplishment I had in watching Quinn do it right. Now I had no idea if he'd ever do it right again in his life, but for that day, I was going to claim victory in his accomplishments . . .

Yesterday in the driveway, Quinn was shooting every shot correctly. I'm no longer coaching basketball, but his new coach is enjoying the fruits of all of my labors. His coach has no idea of what we went through to get Quinn to that point. But the important thing is that Quinn is now doing it right . . . I did my job. That's the way it goes in youth sports . . . I do my job as coach and pass the kids on to the next guy. All of us, coaches, parents, officials, the league, have to realize that ultimately we're on the same team . . . we're working together to get the kids the best youth sports experience possible.

I wonder about all of the things I'm tearing my hair out about right now. Next season they'll naturally get big leads, swing aggressively at the plate, hit the cutoff man, etc. and their coach (if it isn't me) will never know the amount of Rolaids I've consumed this season getting them to that point . . . Oh well, I may not get to taste the fruit, but I can take a little pride and pleasure that I planted the seed, nurtured the tree, and got to watch it grow.

Part V

June

June 1

Confusing Anthony

I confused Anthony at the game last night. He's been in a bit of a slump at the plate lately and his flaw became obvious during his first at-bat: I noticed that most of the time he takes the first pitch. Often he doesn't even look ready in the batter's box; he's already decided he's not going to swing at the first pitch. Last night the bat was on his shoulder and he held it with one hand. The pitcher saw this and threw a strike . . . like many of his at-bats, this put Anthony in a hole.

Before his second at-bat I told him to swing at the first pitch if it was a strike. "Be aggressive and hit the ball hard if it is there," I encouraged. My hope was to change his thinking and get him a good pitch to hit and break him out of the slump. He looked a little confused . . . I should have picked up on that.

He swung meekly at the first pitch and hit a little weak popup in the infield. His father became agitated, and from the stands yelled, "Anthony, what are you doing? Don't swing at that!"

Anthony, and everyone else, heard the pointed question. As he jogged back to the dugout, he looked nervously over at me. After the inning I asked him what happened and he said his father instructed him to be more patient and take the first pitch. Anthony obviously felt caught in the middle — I was telling him one thing and Dad was preaching the complete opposite.

Dad came over to the dugout and politely, but firmly, told me he didn't want Anthony swinging at the first pitch. He had analyzed the statistics and determined Anthony had a very low batting average when he did. I was happy to engage in the strategy/problem-solving discussion with Dad, although I thought it would have been more appropriate to talk before he gave Anthony instruction, not after a wasted at-bat in the fourth inning. I asked him if we could talk after the game.

When we caught up later, I agreed with Dad that taking a strike can be an effective strategy for a struggling hitter, especially if he is impatient and swinging at a lot of bad pitches. But, as a rule, my philosophy was not to take the bat out of a player's hands, and that at some point soon we needed him to feel comfortable swinging at the first pitch. I explained that sometimes the best pitch a hitter will see in an at-bat is the first one, and once the pitcher gets ahead in the count, he may not throw another hittable pitch. And, I concluded, that if Anthony was to continue with this strategy, we needed to work with him on not giving away his intentions.

Both Dad and I kept it positive, which, I suppose meant we both *Responded* well to the situation. We both want Anthony to be more successful at the plate, and we recognize that each of us has an opportunity to help. I could have confronted Dad and told him to back off, but If we argue over a small tactic like this, we run the risk of alienating Anthony and making the game less fun. The kid will feel uncomfortable, always concerned that he's letting one of us down.

But the real issue here isn't about swinging or not swinging at the first pitch. It's not about being right or wrong, either. It's about communication. I don't blame Anthony — he's caught in the middle trying to have fun and be successful. The coach has the responsibility to set expectations, and both coach and parent need to communicate with each other. I probably haven't been clear with parents that I'd like for them to discuss any special strategies, techniques, or fundamentals they are working on with their kids. Most parents aren't giving their kids any instruction — they leave that to the coaches and instead spend their energy being supportive. The best situation is, as coach Sam likes to say, when coaches coach, players play, and parents cheer.

In this case though, Dad does have some knowledge of the game, which I respect. I told him in the future that I'd like for us to communicate better — we may not always agree, but for Anthony's sake, we need to give him one set of instructions. I also gently reminded him that I have a larger responsibility to the team and have to make sure expectations and instructions are consistent. There would be things that I needed Anthony to do a certain way, or in a particular situation, for the benefit of the team. Dad agreed, and we both felt good about things going forward.

Next season I will likely use this as an example in my parent meeting as to how and why parents and coaches need to maintain clear lines of communication. I will be more direct that parents have the responsibility to talk to me first before giving any instruction that may or may not conflict with the team approach.

Mandatory

I was talking to a coaching buddy earlier this morning and he was calling a mandatory parent meeting to cover several team issues and discuss logistics for the out-of-state trip his team is taking next week. Even though he said in the email that it was a mandatory meeting, three parents asked if they had to be there. He said it took every ounce of his strength not to reply sarcastically to each of them.

Some parents like structure and want rules in place . . . as long as they don't have to follow the ones that inconvenience them.

My friend joked that the spelling of the word mandatory should be: man-DUH-tory.

I replied that, just like in the word "team," there is no "I" in "mandatory" . . .

June 6

The Health of a Young Pitcher – Pitch Counts and Curve Balls

"What are you doing to this poor kid?"

I kept asking myself that question at the tournament last weekend as I watched two kids toil on the mound for complete games against us. Each of them threw way too many pitches and one hurled close to 40 curveballs. The other was shaking his arm on the mound in the later innings, obviously feeling fatigue, if not pain. But he stayed in the game. I believe the two coaches risked the kids' health so their teams would have a better chance of winning.

Kids are amazingly resilient, bouncing back from any number of pains and injuries, yet damage to young shoulders and elbows can be severe and permanent. In the blink of an eye or the course of a single season a kid can go from phenom with a future to a kid who can't throw without pain. Maybe I'm more sensitive to this issue because a blown shoulder ended my career, but proper mechanics, pitch counts and curveballs are my three pet peeves when it comes to pitching.

Proper Mechanics

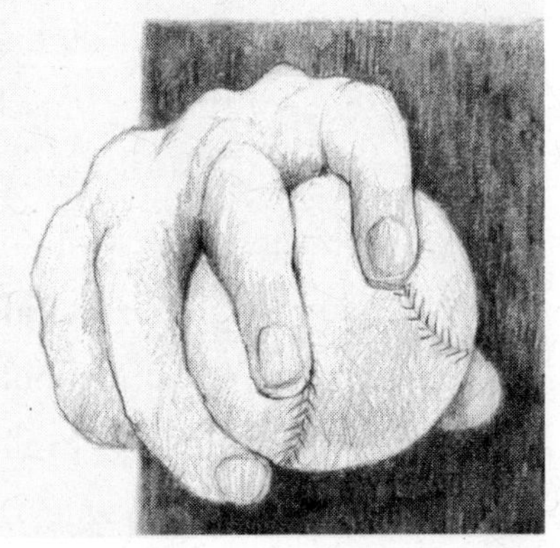

Quite simply, the human arm is not designed to throw a baseball overhand. While underhand is a natural motion, coming over the top or even sidearm puts enormous strain on the shoulder and elbow. Even with the best throwing form, A+ physical conditioning, and strong muscles, throwing a baseball causes wear and tear to the tendons, ligaments, and other soft tissues. That's why major league pitchers get three or four days off in between starts — the arm needs to rest and repair.

Many kids, though, have never been taught to throw correctly and their form is, at best, inefficient and at worst, causing damage to the shoulder or elbow. Current research in the orthopaedic community seems to indicate that poor throwing mechanics are responsible for many injuries in youth sports — perhaps even as much as overuse and throwing curveballs, which get much more attention.

The "drop and drive" technique I learned was state of the art 25 or 30 years ago. But an alarming number of injuries, surgeries, and wrecked careers have led to more healthy mechanics for both young and mature pitchers. Proper throwing technique, unfortunately, is not innate. You don't just pick up a ball and glove and have good form . . . it must be taught and continually reinforced.

Well-meaning dads having a catch with their kid can unwittingly reinforce bad mechanics with a simple, "Wow, that one really cracked the glove!" Soon a kid is contorting his whole body, placing enormous strain on his arm to get a little extra pop on his throws and obtain the praise. And thus the bad habit is off and running, to be reinforced with every subsequent throw. Muscle memory quickly takes over and the kid knows no other way of throwing. Breaking him of this poor form requires enormous physical and mental retraining by a committed coach who knows proper technique.

The solution? Coaches should learn, teach, and continually reinforce proper throwing mechanics to all of their players. Its very easy to fall into bad habits without realizing it — even professional pitchers get constant reminders from pitching coaches to maintain proper mechanics. Youth coaches need to be vigilant about the throwing form of their players both while warming up and in games. One of the pitchers we faced over the weekend looked like he was getting tired and he changed his throwing motion to compensate. It was a double whammy of bad mechanics and a tired arm — a recipe for injury.

Pitch Counts

In game one of the tournament last Saturday the opposing 12-year-old threw 117 pitches in six innings. In game two, it was an 11-year-old throwing 108 pitches in five innings, about 40 percent of which were curveballs. That's far too many for a kid to throw. Period. His growing muscles, bones, and joints can't handle that much use.

Knowledgeable people have studied this. The American Sports Medicine Institute, The Little League®, and many other organizations have set guidelines for the number of pitches a kid should throw and the days off needed in between games he'll pitch. The range for 11- to 12-year-olds is about 65 to 85 pitches with two or three days of rest. The Little League® adopted these guidelines as rule in 2007. Deservedly, they've received widespread praise.

Unfortunately, though, many leagues and most tournaments still measure the wrong thing. They only limit the number of innings a kid can pitch. Innings are a poor indicator of the stress to a players arm, and they allow a coach to overuse his pitchers and hide within the loopholes of loose regulations.

Here's the problem. José pitches three innings, making 41 throws to the plate, while his counterpart in the other dugout, Willie, has thrown 89 pitches in those same three innings.

- The league says each kid can pitch three more innings.
- José's coach says, "One more inning, José. No problem."
- Willie's coach says to himself, "We're losing, so I might as well try to get another inning or two from Willie so I can save Jeff for tomorrow's game."
- The orthopaedic surgeon who, next week, may get to see Willie in his office is screaming, "Are you out of your mind? You're on the verge of inflicting serious, if not irreparable damage to this kid's shoulder and you want to squeeze another inning out of him? I don't care if the game is on the line or it's what's best for the team. His arm is shot. Where is Child Social Services when you need them?"

It happens more than we think. It is easy for everyone to turn a blind eye and simply say, "It's not my player, so it's not my business." Wrong. When we see something dangerous, we all have a responsibility to all the youth playing the game. If a rattlesnake was on the field, we'd all say something . . . where do we draw the line?

Unfortunately, coaches can't always rely on the kids to speak up when they are tired or hurting. Many will ignore fatigue or discomfort to get the opportunity to pitch. They want the ball. I know I always did . . . the possibility of permanent injury seemed outlandish to my adolescent mind.

The other teams' manipulation of the pitch counts over the weekend isn't an aberration. Sadly, it is becoming mainstream.

Overuse injuries among youth athletes are an epidemic in the United States. Even the *Wall Street Journal* had a recent article about the explosion of these types of preventable injuries. It's not uncommon for some teams to play 70 or 80 games in five months. Setting aside the obvious danger of mental burnout, there's a serious physical toll associated with that much repetitive motion. And many kids in warm-weather states endure this punishment year-round, greatly increasing the likelihood of catastrophic damage.

A common repetitive motion injury is "Tommy John Syndrome" in which the ulnar collateral ligament in the elbow is damaged. Named after the major league pitcher who first had the surgery to resurrect his **should-be**-Hall-of-Fame career, Tommy John surgery replaces the ligament in the elbow with a tendon from elsewhere in the body. Nationwide, this is an epidemic. Orthopaedic surgeons are aghast at the number of such injuries and scores of teenagers undergo the procedure every year.

The solution is clear: count and limit pitches. It's the only reliable way to protect kids from themselves and from coaches who are, at best, unknowledgeable and, at worst, focused only on winning.

Curveballs

Make no mistake, at the youth level, curveballs can be a devastating pitch. They're usually effective because most kids haven't seen them very often and have trouble adjusting to the slower speed and movement of the ball down and across the strike zone. There's also a "scare" factor of a spinning ball threatening to hit them in the arm . . . it too can be pretty powerful.

So kids try to throw breaking balls . . . and often they work. So the kid keeps throwing curves . . . and has more success. Soon he's forgotten about developing a strong fastball or change up and is hooked on the hook.

Curveballs, though are dangerous to a young arm. Throwing a breaking ball requires the pitcher to flip his wrist to spin the ball so that the laces will bite against the air in a uniform way and eventually change the ball's trajectory. This turning or flipping of the wrist impacts all of the muscles, tendons, and ligaments from the hand to the shoulder. And if not done precisely the right way, with the correct angle of the arm, it puts tremendous strain on the elbow and shoulder. Until a young pitcher's growth plates fully mature, the arm is at risk from such forces. The damage can be severe and often irreversible.

Growing up I played with a couple of kids who did more than experiment with curveballs and sliders. By the time they reached early high school they couldn't throw without pain and their pitches no longer had competitive velocity. Poof — career over.

While there are correct ways to throw a curve ball that does not put damaging strain on the arm, most kids can't perfect that proper throwing motion. Go watch any group of kids throw between the ages of eight and 13 and you'll be hard pressed to find any who have a healthy overhand form to produce the proper arm angles. And even if you find a specimen ready for it today, kids are moving targets. They're growing so fast at these ages that the body they owned in March is a smaller, lighter, and weaker version of their June form. They have a constantly changing sense of strength, coordination, and flexibility that can make it difficult to safely walk and chew gum at the same time, let alone perfect a complicated pitching motion that even professionals struggle to maintain.

I'll admit a few can probably do it safely. They possess the necessary body control, have been taught the right mechanics, and are under the supervision of a knowledgeable pitching coach. However, the vast majority of young pitchers don't possess all three, and as a result, put their futures at risk by throwing curveballs. Once damaged, they are usually done, unless they have the desire and resources to try the last-ditch option of surgery.

And all of this for what? Win this one game in April? Be a great pitcher at age 12 . . . and then out of the sport by 15? Build a reputation to eventually catch a scout's attention? Really . . . is it worth it? In fact, many professional scouts are starting to shy away from players who threw lots of curveballs early in their careers. They realize that while the arm may look healthy, it could just be a matter of time before injuries start popping up on these kids.

Learning to throw a change up is a much healthier option, and one that will make them effective at 12 and a master of the pitch at 16. A change up is gripped differently but thrown with the same motion as a fastball, which doesn't turn the wrist. Because change ups usually take longer for a pitcher to perfect, youth leagues are excellent proving grounds for how and when to throw them. By comparison, curve balls are easier to learn and can be taught in high school (or later) when the health risk is much less. And, hopefully, they'll be taught by pitching coaches who should know the correct mechanics.

The solution? Outlaw curveballs in leagues with players 13 and younger. Teach the change up. A league in Massachusetts did this more than 15 years ago . . . they now have virtually no arm problems among their pitchers. Umpires are trained to watch for spinners and after two warnings the kid is removed from the game. It can and should be done.

While the kids are the ones who make the pitches and throw the curves, it is the coach who determines how many, when, and why. The problem with this system became clear to me in our third game of the weekend. It started when the opposing coach wouldn't even shake my hand during the meeting with the umpires, preferring to stare silently with a look of superiority on his face. I glanced over his shoulder and saw his team warming up and doing calisthenics with precision that would have brought a tear to a Marine drill sergeant's eye. Their dugout was immaculate — every bag was hung on the back at the exact same height and distance from each other. Later, his team jogged in from the outfield in two neat rows of six players each, almost in perfect step with each other. The coach's arrogance oozed from the entire organization.

I had to admit, at least at first, this gaudy show of discipline was impressive. But I soon wondered what price they paid for it. I have my team practicing, at best, twice a week for two hours each. In those four hours we work on fundamentals, making sure each kid can catch ground balls and fly balls and then know where to throw them. We work on hitting and our pitchers throw. When time permits we do base running and cover basic defensive plays. To get 12-year-olds to master this — and then show the synchronization of a drill team — seems to be a 20-hour a week commitment. I mean, they are 12 . . . I've seen a 12-year-old's room . . . and bathroom. Discipline isn't exactly innate for most of them. So what did this coach — or more accurately, the kids and their families — have to forego to learn this level of perfection? No, I figured, my job wasn't to prepare them for a career in the military … it was to teach them to love the game and play better baseball.

Sadly, when I look around at any of the tournaments we've played in, or even in our league, I can easily spot a few of these coaches. They are the minority, but they have a powerful influence on their peers.

Just win, baby.

And they often do.

If I had kids for 20+ hours a week and wasn't concerned about their long-term physical or mental health, I might be able to develop an equally impressive program. Guys like we saw over the weekend, though, aren't in it for the kids. They're in it for themselves. They simply want the world to believe they are the best coach on the planet.

Despite what grandiose scenarios these guys might have rattling around in their heads, here's the reality: major league managers like Tony La Russa, Dusty Baker, and Joe Girardi do not comb through The Little League® ranks looking for a bench coach. College skippers aren't either, and very few high school coaches are looking to youth coaches to fill staff vacancies. A few good ones might make the jump to coach a freshman team, but only if there isn't a qualified teacher looking for the opportunity.

Tragically though, his winning record almost ensures that this ego-driven coach has an endless supply of talent. He overuses his pitchers to beat coaches and teams who have equal talent but more scruples. With a well-oiled recruiting infrastructure in place, he can be as cavalier as he wants with players and families. If Jimmy develops a sore arm and the doctor tells him to take three months off, the coach simply calls the parents at the top of his list of families anxious for their kid to be able to play on a renowned program with a coach that has such an impressive win-loss record. His success over this 80 game season, though, is much like that of the owners of textile mills in the early 1900's who achieved great wealth through the brutal toil of sweatshop labor. Jimmy is simply collateral damage and soon forgotten. While the juggernaut rolls on, another body limply falls to the side of the road . . . the innocent dreams and spirit of youth tragically crushed.

The solution? This one is tough for coaches to police. Obviously we can each do our part with our teams, but outside of that we have little control. When we see a colleague sending his 10-year-old back out to the mound for his 91st pitch, we should say something. Although powerless to stop it, we can raise awareness and set expectations.

Ultimately though, it's up to parents. They have to honestly answer some important questions:

- Is winning really that important?
- Do we need an 80-game schedule?
- Is the coach overusing pitchers?
- How many kids have sore arms?
- How many kids left the team last year?
- Why did they leave?
- Is he teaching kids to throw the curveball and/or encouraging them to throw it in games?

Limiting pitches and outlawing curveballs will improve safety but, quite simply, parents need to get more involved. Drive-by participation won't cut — it not when the physical and mental health of our kids is at stake. Only parents can squelch the talent pipeline and stop the advance of these arrogant winning machines that shamelessly chew up and spit out the dreams of young ballplayers. Parents must be vigilant, knowledgeable, and aware.

Okay, glad to get that off my chest. Life can now go on.

Sliding at Second – Part 5

Ap · o · plec · tic *(adjective). Furious; exhibiting symptoms of stroke.*

I've always wanted to use the word *apoplectic*, but it seems so extreme for most situations. I never had reason to express such ultimate frustration. I do now. Officially, I now become apoplectic when the kids don't slide at bases.

I lost it with Alan at the game yesterday. After a solid single to left, I had him steal second. He didn't slide and he was out on a close play. As he ran back towards the dugout I gave him an angry, disbelieving look and said, as calmly as I could muster, "You have to slide, Alan. You have to. You just have to," I pleaded. "What can I say to you so that you get it?"

I was way past my boiling point on this issue. I was apoplectic.

We've practiced it several times. We've talked about it. I've explained the need for it. I have laughed with them about it. I have pleaded with them about it. I've been tossed out of a game for arguing about it. I have even yelled at them about it. I make a point of asking them in a joking way before each game, "Again, guys, what is it that we do at second base?" I get a chorus of, "Slide, coach," half with laughs, half with groans.

Alan continued his slow, disgraced trot back to the dugout.

"What will it take?" I repeated.

He shrugged his shoulders. I didn't know what else to say, but could feel the blood vessels in my temples throbbing . . . they were about to burst. That is what apoplectic feels like.

Finally I blurted, "Go give me 20 pushups." It's all I could think of in that moment that didn't involve medieval torture equipment.

He gazed at me with a "You serious, coach?" look.

"You heard me. Go out behind the dugout in the grass and give me 20 pushups," I growled. On a roll now, I stood in front of the dugout and proclaimed that for the rest of the season anyone not sliding at a base when they were supposed to would have to immediately give me 20 pushups. I told them that I didn't care what it looked like or what other people thought about it, we would do things right and slide at bases.

"It's embarrassing for you to not be sliding," I explained, trying to hide most, but not all of my frustration. "Eight-year-olds CAN do it. Eight year olds ENJOY doing it.

"It is a simple fundamental that we've talked about again and again. You guys, for some reason, refuse. It is costing us base runners. Alan was out because he didn't slide. Now we have to start the rally all over again. His nice hit was just erased by a mental mistake." I concluded, "It's the same result as if he had struck out." I wheeled around and headed back to the coaching box to calm down.

Oh, the humanity.

Breathe . . . *Respond* . . .

Unbelievably, two other players had to give me pushups during the game.

I need to ask them why they aren't sliding because I've instructed, explained, and reinforced. I'm, in a word, apoplectic. I'd even be thrilled with a stop, drop, and roll at this point!

Maybe I'm just trying to access the same part of the 12-year-old brain that is also responsible for cleaning their rooms, not leaving dishes on the sofa, doing their chores, picking up the living room . . .

June 9

Dillon on Cloud Nine

Tonight was a great moment in youth sports. Nobody will see it on ESPN or read about it in *Sports Illustrated.* It was a smaller, but still quite meaningful moment that will last at least three lifetimes — Dillon's, his dad's, and mine. Tonight, we fully ignited Dillon's passion for the game and he officially became a baseball junkie. I'll reflect back on this with a warm smile when I'm old and gray in the nursing home (assuming I have memories at that point . . . I may just have a warm smile and pudding on my face . . .).

Dillon is on cloud nine after a fantastic game, helping us on the mound and at the plate get a dramatic win against our cross-town rivals. I brought him in to relieve Tyler who had worked himself into a bases-loaded no-out jam. It was the bottom of the third and we were clinging to a 3 - 2 lead. This was pressure! Dillon struck out the first two batters he faced, walked in a run, and then got a pop up to end the inning. He gave up only one run in what could have been a disaster of an inning for us.

Dillon sprinted off the field with an enormous smile on his face. He knew he had done a great thing, not only as an individual performer, but he'd made an important contribution to his team. He received pats on the back and high fives from his teammates as he entered the dugout. Later, in the sixth inning he got a hit and scored an important insurance run. Then in the bottom of the inning, he took a relay throw from the outfield and fired it to third base to double up a runner trying to advance. This dramatic, heads-up play ended the game, but it was his solid pitching and timely hitting that gave us the win tonight. After the game his body language told the story: head high, chest out and confident stride.

Dillon has had a season of smiles so far. It's been rewarding to see him regain and grow his passion for baseball. He's a kid with a strong throwing arm and talent for the game, but he has a wide range of interests. He could have given up on the game if he had another frustrating season and negative experience with coaches. Until tonight, that is. We — the larger baseball community — now have him for life. After tonight, baseball will never again just be an activity. It will be a passion. It will be played with gusto and the game will be respected for what it is and what it has to offer. He now sees it as a way to learn about himself as a competitor, how to handle success and failure, and how to work hard and enjoy a sense of accomplishment. That's not possible with a mere activity — only a passion can do that.

For most kids, the passion is already there . . . we need to nurture it, feed it and give it room to grow. Our job is to show them the possibilities of what the game has to offer, and then let the passion flourish. This is our opportunity and our legacy as coaches. Dillon is a mark in my personal win column.

June 12

Sliding at Second – Part 6

After the game last night I was talking to a group of parents, basking in the glow of a 13 - 5 victory. We replayed the big hits and commended Bobby for his pitching performance. Eventually though, the topic turned to the three kids who did pushups for not sliding at a base.

I suppose it was inevitable the conversation would head in that direction. Parents are just as confounded as I am. None of us can understand how the kids — nearly all of them — fail to slide. It's one of the most simple, fundamental things to do in baseball, yet we can't seem to get it done.

"You had three kids get to work on upper-body strength and conditioning," said Glen. The sheepish grin on his face indicated he was fully aware that his comment had the same effect as poking me in the ribs with a sharp stick. I may have involuntarily flinched at the thought, but the only reply I could muster was to shake my head in disbelief.

Kate added, "None of them even seemed phased by having to do pushups."

"Nope," I said, continuing to shake my head from side to side. "I didn't even have to tell Jaime. He just ran past me and started doing his 20."

Glen tried to break the gloom this topic was having on our conversation. "Well, they say if you're going to do the crime, you have to be willing to do the time," he said with a laugh.

"That's what I mean!" exclaimed Kate, also giggling with a strange combination of smile and astonishment on her face. "They all seem willing to do the time — the punishment is just part of the game now."

I pondered that for a moment, considering the wisdom of my reward and punishment system. "Yeah, we seem to have a bunch of hardened criminals," I lamented aloud. "I'm going to start calling our dugout C-block."

We all laughed and then agreed on a place to go have dinner.

I'm glad I have the parents' support on this because it has certainly become an issue that makes me question my effectiveness as a coach. I mean, if I can't get them to execute this one simple thing how can I expect to teach them anything?

I know, I can't think that way. The kids are the ones that have to step up and do it . . . but that realization doesn't neutralize all of the acid pooling in my stomach . . .

June 13

A Mom and Her Pictures

Youth sports focuses far too much on the end result and overlooks the value of the experience of simply playing the game. It is, after all, just a game . . . a great game . . . a game meant to be enjoyed for its own sake, not the material things winning may promise (like championship trophies, perceived status of winning, or college scholarships). Too many of us adults get blinded by adult motivations. We seem to value most winning and the promise of playing at the next level, whatever that might be.

From this adult perspective, what's the value of my 15 years of playing organized competitive baseball? I didn't play professional ball and I'm sure the dollars my parents shelled out in all of those years totaled more than the value of my college scholarship. So, again, what's the value of my baseball career? It's a voyage that took me further than 99 percent of all kids who played ball as a 12-year-old. The final destination certainly wasn't of value to me . . . three shoulder surgeries, the loss of a scholarship, and a year of wandering through college trying to figure out what else there was in life besides the incredible thrill of throwing a baseball past a hitter.

It is now clear to me that, like many things in life, the value of youth baseball is in the journey, not the destination. On that scale, my career has tremendous value — but mostly to me. The significance is in the friendships I made, the laughs I enjoyed, experiencing accomplishment and defeat, the fun I had, the characters I met, and from time to time, the excellence I achieved. My memories are rich and the game taught me life lessons I couldn't have learned any other way. That's value. THAT is why we should want our kids to play the game.

When we reach 40 years old, the important things aren't going to be how many wins we accrued or if we played varsity ball. It will be the fond memories we have on the diamond and in the dugout with friends. The value will be in how much fun the journey was and what the game taught us about ourselves along the way. The value is in the moment, not planning for or dreaming about the next step.

I write about this today because several events over the last week reinforce these ideals and made me think about **fun, learn, compete** from a slightly different perspective.

Event #1 (last week)

We were waiting behind the backstop for a 10-year-old game to finish so we could play on the field. It was a good game and the home team had the tying run on third base with nobody out in the last inning. My love for the game drew me in and I quickly became hooked on the unfolding baseball drama. These 10-year-olds were engaged, encouraging each other, standing in the dugout, yelling and cheering as if this was the most important thing in the world at that moment.

And for those adults in the right frame of mind, maybe it was . . . what a release and escape this opportunity provided . . . worries like finances, a mean boss, getting the car into the shop, or an angry neighbor . . . all gone from consciousness at that moment. I was allowing myself to be pulled into that world. I was enjoying it.

But I had the misfortune of overhearing some spectators lamenting the fact that this was merely AA ball. Only then did I notice that the fielders didn't throw very hard and often had trouble catching the ball. The batters didn't swing as hard as the 12-year-olds on Alan's team. The magic of the moment evaporated . . .

When I started thinking like an adult, my mind strayed from the drama of a last-inning rally. My conditioned mind started thinking about which ones might play high school ball. I wondered which ones would have the chance to play AAA next year and if the 10 AAA coaches knew who they were. The enjoyment of this precious baseball moment was swept away with thoughts and value judgments about the future and what it might promise an adult.

These "mature" thoughts devalued that game and those players. I wasn't placing any worth on the baseball drama, simply the level of play and the end result that might produce. As a student of the game, I failed. The game is bigger than those judgments. The players, parents, and coaches were obviously getting the same enjoyment from the game that my 12-year-olds get. Maybe more. Kudos to them.

Event #2 (last Friday)

A coaching friend of mine was driving through the grocery store parking lot with a few players from his AAA team and they stopped to talk to the mom of a kid who played with them last season. This year her son moved up to majors with another team. About two minutes into the conversation she proudly told the coach she was so glad that her son had moved up because he would be so bored at the AAA level. That certainly silenced the carload of AAA players . . . and diminished their efforts. What a mean and classless thing to say.

If I dismiss the play of a AA team, and a majors parent devalues a AAA team, when does it stop? Is there value in any competition below the major league level? Again, I achieved what 99 percent of players never experience in their careers . . . what's the value of my experience?

Unfortunately I think many coaches and parents fall into this trap of trampling the level below them while grasping for the level above. This happens not only in sports but also in academics and most other activities. Even the parents of the kid playing second trumpet are guilty if they feel a certain superiority over the kids playing third and fourth trumpet. It's like an exclusive club and entry requires distancing yourself from the riff raff . . . if you want people talking about you and paying attention to your efforts then you better be winning and be on the high school track . . . or at least talk a good game.

Event #3 (weekend)

I was lucky that Alan's tournament schedule this weekend didn't conflict with my 35+ men's league game, so I got nine innings of hardball in on Sunday. Great therapy!

We've been short on players and our manager added a new guy, Luiz, to the roster who lives about 90 miles away. He's a good player with a great attitude and he'll be a good addition to the team.

It was an exciting game, seesawing back and forth several times. We lost in the bottom of the ninth on a bloop single to right. As we were leaving the field, I said, "Luiz, thanks for driving all the way down here to play with us."

He grinned like a six-year-old on Christmas morning. "Heck," he said, "I'm so happy to be playing again. It's been about 20 years since I played. I got all of those old feelings again. I was even nervous before the game, just like in high school. 90 miles is nothing . . . I'd drive all night for another at-bat or inning at shortstop!"

He paused for a moment, turned to me and said, "Thank you for letting me play."

His words demonstrated only a small portion of his passion for the game. The smile on his face and the enthusiasm in his tone left no doubt he plays the game for the sheer enjoyment of being on the field. He's 38-years-old. He's done with high school, and college ball is a distant memory. He's in no immediate danger of being scouted by a minor league team.

But in Luiz I saw that same passion for playing that I see in most of the kids on my team. He reminded me of what our motivations should be . . . to ignite a fire in our youths and give them the opportunity to play, no matter the level, no matter the future. Just play the game. ***Play for the love of the game.*** Just let them enjoy this opportunity.

Event #4 (weekend)

What brings this issue to mind today was the mother of a player on a weaker AAA team we played in the tournament last weekend. She was struggling to get a good photo of her son batting. Her frustration mounted as she tried to get the best angle, climbing and reaching over the chain link fence. The openings aren't large enough for a lens and the fence was at least six feet tall. She was living proof that it's not easy to be a photographer on most baseball fields.

I invited this mom through the gate and into our dugout where she wouldn't have a fence to look over or through (for some competitive coaches this would be baseball blasphemy to have a mom in the dugout like this). She was very grateful to get that vantage point. As she clicked away I saw that she clearly understood the importance of what she was doing . . . creating a series of photos to augment her son's fond memory of his baseball experience.

He was obviously not one of the better players on the field. His team was not winning and if I had to guess, he probably won't play high school ball. Yes, it's still way too early in his career to know for sure, but he lacked fine motor skills and speed. Obviously they could develop in the four years before high school . . . but that's not the point.

The great thing was, this kid was perfectly fine with who he was, where he was, and what he was doing. He clearly had a passion for the game and was taking this opportunity very seriously, trying to improve. He was having fun and enjoying the experience.

The mom didn't care if his team won or lost. She probably wasn't concerned whether or not her son was going to play high school ball. She wasn't bothered by the score of this game. Rather, it was all about this precious moment in time. It was about his experience of playing a game he obviously loved. The level of play wasn't important — only the opportunity to play. And all she seemed to want was for him to enjoy himself. Her photos will trigger a flood of fond memories 30 years from now. That's being a supportive parent.

If we focus only on the end results (winning, high school baseball or college scholarships), what is the value of this mom's efforts? What is the value of her son's experience? It gets lost, ignored and completely devalued by the discussion about who won the tournament and which kids are high school material. Is his experience any more or less valuable than Alan's? Is it any more or less valuable than the stud pitcher's that we faced the day before? They're all kids playing a game . . . let them focus on that. The other issues will sort themselves out when they get to high school.

But if we look at the process, that kid is getting just as much — if not more — from the experience than most of the other kids out there. He's taking it seriously, he's learning, he's competing, he's making the most of an opportunity, and he's having fun. If we look at the events of today 30 years from now, none of the kids are going to be playing professional baseball, and most of them won't have played varsity in high school. But who will have the fondest memories? Who will look back and smile? Who will have received the most value from their experience?

I give kudos to that mom and that kid. They smelled the roses and valued that moment. I'm glad they were playing and glad they were enjoying the experience. They made a conscious effort to be in a position to have fun, learn, and be competitive.

That's what youth sports should be about. Stop planning and start playing. Savor the moments.

Treat it as both the most important thing in the world at that instant and as an activity without consequences where the outcome is meaningless. Value the endeavor, not the results. Celebrate the effort and drama on the field. Enjoy what we have today — the future will take care of itself . . . and our kids will be too old soon enough. Too bad most adults don't see the opportunity right in front of them.

And, I suppose when all else fails, and the road ahead isn't clear, adults should just get the heck out of the way and let the kids enjoy their game.

June 15

My Grandma's Fantastic Memory

Unlike most people, my grandma's memory has gotten better with age. The secret isn't green tea or gingko biloba. It just seems that the older she gets, the better ballplayer I was growing up. Her memories of my performance, like fine wine, have improved over time.

We took her to Alan's game last night. At 92-years-old, she's amazingly sharp and still loves to watch a ballgame, especially if her great-grandson happens to be playing third base. She's the most loyal and vocal fan around, letting coaches and umpires know what she thinks of their performance.

Her baseball legacy began in the 1920s growing up with two sports-loving brothers and a tomboy sister (one brother played in the Orange Bowl and enjoyed a year of professional football). My grandma played all sports but baseball was her favorite. She describes herself as a slick-fielding second baseman but "couldn't hit to save my neck." Later she dutifully kept score for her three sons' teams while my grandpa coached. She went to every game; cold, wind, rain, sun, or snow never dampened her spirit or desire to sit and root for her favorite ballplayers. Her love for baseball lay dormant until I was old enough to play. Making up for lost time, she attended most of my youth and high school games, again logging balls, strikes, and outs in her scorebook.

She knows the game well, and last night she shared several stories about my grandpa, dad, two uncles, and me with Bev, her parents, my parents, and everyone else behind the backstop. I could overhear her narration as I stood outside the dugout, and, as she described my exploits on the field, I had no idea I was that dominating on the mound, so feared at the plate, and so flawless in the field. To hear her tell it, I walked on water . . . revisionist history never sounded so good!

In between the third and fourth innings I stood along the fence between home and third base talking to Glen, one of the parents on the team. We both stopped to listen to my grandma finish a story about a game I played in high school. While I can't prove it didn't happen the way she described it, my recollection of that game was decidedly different. But I was flattered. You'd think I'd already be in the Hall of Fame with as much skill as she gave me credit for having.

Glen had a "Wow, that's impressive" look on his face.

I turned to him with a red face and confessed, "You know that's not exactly how I remember it."

He smiled, appreciating my candor as well as the love grandma was demonstrating for the game and me. "Gee, Dan, I don't know. Sounds pretty good. You're not going to argue with her, are you?"

I thought about it for a moment, laughed, and agreed. "Yeah, I like her version a lot better than mine!" We both chuckled again.

I'm thankful grandma can come to the games. I know it means a lot to Alan; because of their stages in life, it probably means even more to her. With the vantage point her age and experience afford, she knows better than anyone to cherish these moments. Although separated by almost 80 years, Alan and Grandma's shared passion for baseball melts the age barrier. Alan is old enough to remember her for the rest of his life. I suspect the memories of her that he'll share with his grandkids will be about how she faithfully came to his baseball games. What a great game to bring families and generations together!

June 20

Sliding at Second – Part 7

There are times when, as a competitor, you realize you are overmatched and victory is impossible. Your only strategy at that point is surrender to the moment and accept your defeat with honor. The Samurai calmly bows to his opponent, and, showing great respect, lays down his sword.

I reached this point last night with the sliding at bases issue that I've battled all season. Alan again didn't slide while stealing second base. After he came around and scored on the next play, he dutifully did his 20 pushups behind the dugout.

A few plays later Brandon stole second and executed a beautiful slide at second, popping up after his lead foot hit the base. The throw from the catcher was wild, flying into right-center field, and Brandon raced towards me at third. Although I was yelling, "Down, down, down!" and motioning him to slide, he came in standing up just ahead of the throw. But his momentum carried him just past the base and the third baseman tagged him out.

All I could do was look at him, shake my head and say, "Go give me 20."

I've laid down my sword. I'll refill my bottle of Rolaids and try again next season.

June 21

A Sad Ending to a Friendship

I'm discovering that no matter how strong you think a friendship might be, coaching youth sports puts it at risk. The issues on and off the field are filled with emotions, frustrations, and egos . . . it is a powder keg waiting for a spark to explode. I think my friendship with Robert may have detonated the other day.

The conflict started about a week ago as I asked both assistant coaches separately what they wanted for next season. Sam engaged in the conversation; Robert wouldn't. He abruptly changed the subject. I suggested that they each talk to their families about what would be best for their sons next season and we'd continue the dialogue.

The next day Sam and I had a further conversation. His son Nick is certainly capable of competing at the majors level and Sam said they were onboard with a bigger challenge. It sounded like Sam and his family had a good discussion.

Alan and I have also had good dialogue over the past couple of weeks. I want him to own the decision, so I've asked him a lot of questions, and I've tried to mostly listen. Like me, he's conflicted. He really likes the kids on the team and the chemistry we have. I do too. However, he's also frustrated that we aren't more competitive. Alan does very well against the

AAA pitchers we face, and his batting average for the season is currently .462. His success has earned him the right to move up if he wants. A big part of my decision is based on what Alan wants — every parent has to start there.

A couple of days after Sam and I talked, I finally did get a conversation with Robert and told him of Alan's decision. Robert seemed very angry. It was a heated phone call.

The central issue is that Alan and I decided he will move up from AAA to majors next season. My son has worked hard and had plenty of success at AAA; he is ready for and wants the additional challenge.

However, Robert's son Kaleb has struggled all season at AAA and, in my opinion, isn't ready move up. He's overmatched at the plate, makes more than his share of errors in the field, and shows many signs of frustration. I feel awful for Kaleb because he doesn't appear to be having fun or success. He's a great kid in a bad spot.

Robert told me he feels it is unfair to Kaleb and others to take some of the kids up to the majors level. He believes the team should stay together. He told me that when I sign up to be a coach I have a responsibility to "coach the kids for life." He also believes I have gone behind his back to exclude him from the team next year — he feels I am stealing the team from him. I know Robert is disappointed, but I believe he's *Reacting* to a narrow slice, and it appears he's allowing his ego, anger, and frustration to dictate his actions, all in the name of wanting continuity and comfort for his son.

From my perspective, the facts are this:

Our kids grow up, and they do it at different rates. Nothing stays the same for very long. They develop unique skills and abilities at varying velocities and as they grow their interests and desires take them in different directions. As much as we might like to at times, we can't stop this from happening. You see it happen in academics, music, and other sports. Baseball is no different; the kids who were the best players at age seven aren't always the best players at age 10. Socially, their best friends at age five may not be the kids they hang out with at age 10 or 16. Their interests diverge. That's okay. That's life.

As a result of these growth patterns, I can't be, as Robert says, their coach for life. Unfortunately, the team can't stay together. I'll lose at least a couple of kids no matter what I do. If I move up to majors there will be several kids who aren't ready. However, if I stay at AAA at least two, maybe four, will go find a majors team.

Since our phone conversation, Robert's behavior has turned passive-aggressive — he will not talk to Sam or me. He has refused to coach first base during the last two games and sat quietly at the end of the bench. I think he believes he's hurting me with his silent treatment, but to me he's simply behaving badly in front of the kids and other nine families on the team.

I have valued my friendship with Robert for six years. We've had a lot of great times, including vacationing together. The possibility of losing it to something this trivial is disappointing. The thing that saddens me the most is that he believes my intentions are sinister. I can honestly say that my heart has been in the right place. I'm glad that I spent the time talking to Alan and asked him questions to stimulate his thinking about next season. This clarity of purpose has helped me deal with Robert's behavior in a more balanced and productive way.

However, despite what Robert says, my first responsibility is to my son — if I don't do what is right for Alan, then nobody will. The other families on the team aren't going to change their life direction to accommodate Alan — nor should they. Holding Alan back at AAA because that might be best for Kaleb is unfair. *Would it be fair to Kaleb if Alan failed math and we asked Kaleb to repeat the class with him?*

Ultimately every parent needs to make a decision about what is right for his or her kid. They have to analyze what situation would be best and go in that direction. If everyone does that, there's plenty of room to assemble a team around this common ground. In that respect, nobody steals a team . . . people gravitate to the situation and coach that best meets their needs. Even if it means I'll lose a good player, I encourage parents to do what is best for their kids.

I will give Robert some space. Sometimes we all need a little time to process what is happening. Robert has been a good friend. I hope he'll come around.

The Successful Project

The carrot and the stick both can motivate behavior. Over the last week, I've seen how the carrot can provide a positive lasting impact to a 12-year-old where the stick will just leave a scar. I made a deal with Zach a week ago that if he could have a positive attitude and give me 100 percent effort I would give him a huge reward: to be the starting pitcher in our next-to-last game of the season. It worked. Not only did he have an experience that he'll remember for the rest of his life, but he may have learned how to more effectively deal with frustration and failure — skills that will help him in all sports and in life.

Zach is the youngest player on our team, but what he lacks in size and strength he makes up with hustle and determination. He's a great kid with a disarming shyness and smile that don't always conceal a sharp wit. Zach is third on the team in runs batted in, and he has about as many RBIs as hits, which means every hit has been a big one for us. He's come through in several big situations, delivering the winning blow. He's played catcher, outfield, and second base this season, but his true love is pitching. The problem is that, at this age at least, he doesn't yet have the arm strength or physique to be effective at AAA. I have eight other kids who can pitch on the team, so he hasn't really gotten the chance. I've had him pitch a few times this season, usually in mop-up situations where we're already down a bunch of runs. It's clear though, he's wanted, more than anything, to get a start this season. That's the carrot.

The stick hasn't worked with Zach this season. He's strong-willed and expects perfection from himself; when he doesn't deliver he gets angry and frustrated. He'll hit a hard line drive at the second baseman for an out and storm back to the bench and stew for an inning. He doesn't realize that he had a good at-bat — he simply hit the ball right at someone. He respects the game enough that he doesn't throw his bat or helmet, but he looks angry enough to give them a good toss. This tailspin of despair often takes him out of the game for an inning or two — mentally he's locked up and can't get past the failure. I've tried talking to him about it, reasoning through the failure, processing the anger and threatening to bench him until the attitude turns around. I've had to follow through on that a couple of times, but I haven't seen lasting change. So it was time to try something new with Zach.

Last Tuesday I pulled him aside before our game for a quick conversation.

"Zach, you know we've been talking all season about how we need you to keep a positive attitude even when you fail, right?" I asked as we stood in the outfield grass watching his teammates hit wiffle balls.

"Yeah, coach," he said, looking at the ground, trying to hide some embarrassment with his trademark shyness.

"You know baseball is a game of dealing with failure — we've talked about that. Even the best major league hitters make an out two out of every three times to the plate. How am I going to get you to change your attitude when you get frustrated?"

"I don't know, coach," he mumbled.

I paused for a moment to let him think it through. "How about this," I suggested. "We have tonight's game, one on Thursday, and then the tournament this weekend. That's at least five games. I'll make you a deal. If you can have a good attitude and support your teammates no matter how you are doing individually, I'll give you the ball for Monday's game against the Panthers."

Zach quickly looked up and stared me in the eye.

I confirmed, "Yeah, you'll be the starting pitcher Monday. But that's only if I see a healthier attitude for all five games. If I see you sitting at the end of the bench steaming at yourself for striking out then the deal is off. But if you can learn to turn around the frustration through the next five games, the start is yours."

His smile was enormous. He didn't know what to say.

"Do we have a deal?" I asked, already knowing the answer.

"You bet, coach!"

"You know what behavior I'm looking for, right?"

"Yeah!" he said, still beaming with excitement.

"Okay then, let's see it. All five games, right?"

"Yeah, coach!"

"All right. We have a deal. Now go take some swings and let's get ready to play this game," I said, pointing to the net and wiffle balls strewn down the right field line. After the game I started to explain the deal to Zach's dad and he stopped me mid-sentence, "Zach's already told me about it. Sounds great. Thanks!" I guess Zach was so excited he ran up into the stands before the game and spilled the beans.

Over the weekend Zach upheld his end of the bargain, although once after striking out I had to call his name and stare at him for a moment to remind him of his behavior and the deal. He quickly regained his composure. It's a tough job as a coach to find the right motivation to get through to a kid. The stick of benching him for an inning only brought out his stubbornness . . . the carrot brought awareness and a willingness to change.

We played at 7:30 on Monday evening and I'm sure Zach was the first kid to the park. If his dad had let him spend the night in a tent at the field, he would have done it to make sure he didn't miss his big opportunity. The team warmed up as usual in the grass area next to the diamond while the early game wrapped up. At 7 p.m. I pulled Zach and the starting catcher aside. As I unwrapped the new Rawlings ball, I told Zach to relax, throw strikes and have fun. I gave the shiny sphere a quick rub down.

"The game is now in your hands, Zach," I said. "We're counting on you." I then carefully placed the ball in Zach's outstretched hand and said, "Take good care of this," implying more than simply keeping it white until game time.

At 7:30 Zach took the field, obviously nervous, but eager to get some outs. He got hit pretty hard in the first inning, giving up a walk, two solid singles, and then the right fielder badly misplayed a line drive and the second baseman booted a ground ball. This loaded the bases and Zach was frustrated so I jogged out to the mound to settle him down, as I would with any pitcher in that situation.

"Zach, you're doing exactly what we need right now," I said with a big grin.

"Coach, they're hitting me and we're already losing," his anger mounting. He hadn't been perfect and it wasn't going as well as he'd hoped. He was certain he was failing and thought I might pull him right then.

"All you can do is throw strikes, Zach," I said in a calming tone. "That happens as a pitcher. You've had some tough luck. We should have been out of the inning, but we're not. You have to focus even harder right now and make some good pitches and give your defense a chance to help. They're going to back you up."

I looked around the huddle and Brandon patted him on the back. "Come on Zach," he said. "Get me a ground ball and we'll get out of this."

"We're behind you Zach. This is your game. Go get them," I said, turning back toward the dugout.

They got one more hit in the inning, but Zach relaxed and got out of the jam, giving up a total of four runs.

Our offense clawed right back, scoring three in the bottom half and Zach looked a little more confident only down a run. He set them down one, two, three in the second inning, but we didn't score either and the score remained 4 - 3 going to the top of the third.

As his teammates started to take the field, Zach looked at me quizzically. "Am I going back out there, coach?"

With my best poker face I looked confused, and, in a slightly agitated tone, asked, "What do you mean?" I let that hang in the air for a moment. He immediately realized a pitcher doesn't ask that question. I smiled and explained, "A pitcher goes until the coach takes the ball from him." He nodded and sprinted back out to the mound.

In the third we committed a couple of costly errors and they scored three more runs. Zach walked slowly off the field after we got the third out. His head was down and he knew I'd be taking him out because he'd reached his pitch limit. He went to the end of the bench and sat down, staring at the dugout floor in front of him. He didn't look angry, just dejected.

I walked over and sat next to him, put my hand on his shoulder and said, "Nice game Zach. You battled well. Your defense didn't help you there but I'm proud of the way you kept working hard and you've kept us in the game. We're going to come back and win this."

"But I gave up all those runs!" he blurted. He'd held it in for a while but the frustration and disappointment started to spill out of this fragile young pitcher. It was his big opportunity and it had not gone as planned. The reality of his performance, as well as that of his teammates, didn't feel the way he'd dreamed it up all week. The experience didn't match his expectations.

"That's not your fault," I said sternly. "You did your job. You threw strikes. That is what a pitcher does. A pitcher has to ignore everything that happens to him and focus on the next pitch, the next batter, the next out," I explained, my tone softening to reinforce I was proud of him. "That's what I saw you do. You gave up some hits and were a little wild at times, but you threw a good game. Now, you need to focus on what you can do to help your team win. We need your bat. You're up fifth this inning. You can give yourself a chance to be the winning pitcher. If we come back and take the lead, the win is yours."

Zach considered those facts for a moment and simply said, "Okay coach," and started putting on his batting gloves.

We scored six runs in the bottom of the third inning, which included Zach's two-run double that tied the score. We won 16 - 8 and Zach got the win and had three hits and four RBIs. After the game our team huddled in the grass behind the dugout and I tossed the game ball to Zach, announcing to the team and parents what a great job he did. He was one big smile!

Later, as we walked to the parking lot, I pulled Zach aside. "So what did you learn tonight?"

He thought for a moment, but didn't really have any insights. I'm sure he was still buzzing from a potent mixture of emotions and adrenalin.

"Here's what I saw," helping him begin the mental processing I hoped he'd do on his own. "For the last week, you've worked on not letting frustration ruin your game, right?"

"Yes, coach." I had his full attention.

"Did you have fun this last week while you tried that new approach?" I quizzed.

He shrugged his shoulders. "Yeah, I did."

"Was that more fun than when you'd get down on yourself for mistakes?" I was in full cross-examination mode now.

"Yeah, it was, coach," he admitted.

"Did you make more mistakes this last week than before?"

He pondered the question for a moment. "I don't know."

"I don't think so. You actually played better. I checked the scorebook and you've had at least one hit in four of the last five games." I explained.

"So here's what I want you to think about. You changed your mental approach; frustrations didn't get you down. You had more fun and actually improved your performance. And then you had the monster game tonight where you battled adversity, stayed in the game mentally, and won."

I paused for effect, trying to foster more reflection on the events of the last week. "If it were me, I'd try making this they way you play the game from now on."

"Okay, coach. I'll try."

I could tell from his expression that this complicated message hadn't sunk in yet. It would take him a while to process through it. And it'll take a lot of effort from him to make this a habit. However, his eyes are open to a new way of approaching sports and life. Now it will be up to him to do something productive with it. Fortunately, he has a great memory of tonight, which should motivate him to continue down this path. I'm realizing that opportunities like this are why I wanted to coach in the first place. I felt like I made a difference.

And it taught me that the carrot is mightier than the stick.

June 26

A Sad Ending to a Friendship – Part 2

Last night we lost our last game of the season in a very strange contest. We got the first five batters on base and then the Leopards retired the next 18 in order and we lost 9 - 2. The most bizarre and ugliest part of the evening, however, happened after the game.

Our team gathered at the picnic tables overlooking the field to recap the game and discuss next steps — our usual post-game activity. I announced to the team that I would not be coaching a AAA team next year because Alan wanted to challenge himself and move up to majors. After I finished several parents came up to shake hands and thank me for a great season.

That's when Robert's wife Debbie erupted. She began berating me for my decision to not coach the team next season and how that was grossly unfair to her family. As her tone became more hostile and her decibel level began to redline, the other nine families quickly scattered to avoid the disturbing scene.

None went too far though . . . it was a train wreck happening right in front of them. While they didn't want to be in close enough proximity to get showered with flaming debris, a morbid sense of curiosity kept them within listening distance. I can't blame them . . . I'm sure it was pretty good theater!

Because we've been friends for six years, I let Robert and Debbie vent. I understand how difficult it has been for them to watch Kaleb struggle this season. I sympathize with what they've gone through, so I let them spew and tried not to take anything personally.

I suspect that I may have added to their frustration tonight. I had not specifically told Robert that I would be announcing my decision to the team after the game. Although he knew what my decision was and why I was making it, he didn't know when the announcement was coming. I suppose I should have told him (even though he hasn't officially been talking to me). That omission apparently added fuel to the inferno.

And what a spectacular display it was. They both hit me with those same arguments . . . it was unfair to break up the team . . . the players weren't ready for majors . . . it was wrong of me to steal the team . . . it was unfair to not let Kaleb play with his friends.

They then got personal. Robert repeated his belief that a good coach realizes he has a responsibility to every kid . . . a responsibility to coach them for life . . . they need to know you won't abandon them. Debbie said I was selfish and a bad coach. Robert said I was disloyal and cared nothing for the kids.

My frustration level spiked. I felt that for the last couple of weeks I had gone out of my way to understand their position and not push while they were grappling with the issues. I felt that I had *Responded* to Robert's passive-aggressive behavior by not calling him out and forcing the issue. I have given him time and space to figure things out on his own without pressure or confrontation. I have put the friendship above my needs for a cohesive coaching staff, and perhaps even above those of the team.

But darn it, I have given everything to the team this season. I've devoted 20 to 40 hours every week since January. I've frozen in the snow, chapped in the wind, and baked in the sun. I've gone above and beyond to provide what I thought was the right opportunity, the right environment, and the right instruction for every kid. Certainly I've made mistakes along the way and I have long lists of things I would do differently the next time around. So call me a bad coach … everyone gets an opinion . . .

I snapped, though, when Robert said, in a very condescending tone, that I didn't care about the kids. Debbie gave a silent, smug nod of agreement. I *Reacted.* For the first time in their 10-minute diatribe, I raised my voice. I said, "This is crap," forcefully pointing at them and cutting off Debbie's next sentence. "I'm not going to listen to this anymore," I shouted. "You need to grow up. You are being petty. When you want to discuss this in a fair and rational way, I'm happy to have the conversation. Until then, I'm done." Way past my boiling point, I scooped up my ball bag and fungo bat and stormed towards my car.

I was immediately embarrassed for my outburst. None of the parents or players — including Kaleb and Alan — had moved beyond earshot . . . everyone was engrossed, carefully watching the drama from behind their cars.

Debbie followed me across the parking lot, yelling the entire 40 yards to my vehicle. I popped open the trunk and deposited my equipment. She continued to rant while the group of parents in the stall behind my car stood with mouths agape, staring in disbelief.

I slammed the trunk closed and said calmly, "Debbie, this conversation is over."

About that time two other sets of parents came to my rescue. They offered to buy me dinner and a beer. I have to admit such an offer never sounded so good in my life! I enjoyed quenching my thirst and the supportive conversation that followed.

I'm not sure where to go from here. If I felt I had intentionally hurt them or was being unfair then I'd feel awful. But I don't. I'm not even mad, just very, very sad. I'm disappointed in their words and actions and in my own childish outburst. I'm living proof that you have to be vigilant about your own behavior — youth sports can bring out the best and worst in you. Even if you *Respond* for three weeks, a momentary *Reactive* outburst can forever change the situation.

I've given a lot of thought to my responsibility as a coach. Yes, my impact on the kids will reach far beyond this season. They will have memories — good or bad — of this year and how their coach helped or impeded their growth and influenced their ability to enjoy the game.

But I take issue with Robert's belief that I'm their "coach for life." That's not fair or reasonable. I have 11 kids on the team whose abilities are rapidly diverging. How can I do service to any of them by keeping everyone together? How can that possibly be my responsibility — or decision? Parents make that decision. Kids make that decision. Coaches can only provide options.

I will try to help every kid and parent find a good situation next year, whether that is with me or another coach. Ultimately, though, everyone in the system has to study the landscape, do their own soul searching, and determine what's best for them. Then everyone can start comparing notes and reach compromises that will work the following season.

Under Robert's line of reasoning, if I move up then I'm not being fair to those who want to stay at AAA. But that also means that if I stay at AAA, then I'm not being fair to those who are ready to move up. If I kept Alan at AAA is Sam justified in having a similar fit of rage because I'm not being fair to Nick? Would Sam expect me to coach Nick next season if Alan wasn't ready to play at the same level?

Although I enjoy the coaching role, I am first and foremost a parent. Just because I sign up to be a coach doesn't mean I should have to give up my rights as a parent to make decisions for my son. I have to do what is right for Alan. Nobody else is making decisions for their family based on what would be best for Alan.

I think I've bent over backwards this season to not give Alan preferential treatment. He gets rotations in the outfield in addition to his preferred positions at first or third base. He pitches about the same number of innings as the others. I schedule him to play the same amount as every other kid, and I actually have him sit the bench to start the game more often than the others. If we only play four or five innings due to time expiring or run rule, then he's going to play less than the other kids. Fair? I don't know. But I want it clear that I'm not giving him preferential treatment. Those are the decisions of a coach.

But the end-of-the-season decisions are different. They are the decisions of a parent. I'm making choices for my son that will live well beyond an inning or a game. The levels of competition, team environment, coaching staff, etc. are all things I have to consider as a parent. For Robert to say that I should put the needs of his kid, or other kids, above Alan's is ridiculous. That's unfair to me and to Alan. I'm feeling comfortable and at peace with my decisions and actions. I'm just disappointed that apparently it's not enough to salvage the relationship with Robert.

June 27
Email to Parents

The Morning After — Parent Email

This was the email I sent to parents this morning after I explained my plans for next season.

For the announcement after the game, I found it tough to remember everything I wanted to say, so the email was a good way to reinforce what I had said and make sure everyone understood my message. Sometimes people don't always hear the same thing. I thought a follow up email would make my intentions and message clear.

I didn't feel the need to address the ugly scene with Robert and Debbie after the game. Everyone was there and saw what happened. The focus, after all, should be on the kids and the team — not me, Robert, or the parental drama.

Team —

I realize that my announcement last night may have caught most of you by surprise — that certainly was not my intent. I wrestled with the best way to address the issue with the team because I know how much fun all of us have had this season. There's no great way to say, "Things will be different next year." I decided to address it last night for a few reasons:

- ***Several parents have asked and/or hinted about plans for next year.*** *It's on everyone's mind and it is absolutely a fair question. Once I made my decision, there was no reason to string things out. This gives everyone more time to think about their own situation and what would be best for them.*
- ***I wanted to do it in person.*** *It probably would have been easier for me to send out an email, but I know if I were a parent on a team, I'd want to hear it in person. Waiting until the team party in July seemed unnecessary and unfair.*
- ***I wanted everyone to hear it at the same time.*** *Everyone deserves that respect.*

*Let me also say that my decision has not been an easy one. Coaching this season has been one of the best and most rewarding experiences of my life. That's a statement that is **MUCH MORE** reflective of the 11 great kids and their families than it is about me. I knew this was going to be a fun season. You greatly exceeded my expectations in helping create a positive and fertile learning environment where kids could enjoy the game they love. I've appreciated the opportunity to laugh, grimace, cheer, applaud, feel pride, and shake our collective heads in bewilderment. Thank you.*

For the last month I've asked Alan many different times what he wanted for next year. Over that time he's had the chance to think it through from many angles and he's gradually come to a firm decision. He would like to step up the level of competition and challenge himself more by having the opportunity to play on a majors team. I understand and respect his decision and believe that, although he has a lot left to learn and improve upon (for example . . . slide at second base!), he's ready for that challenge — and that he's earned that opportunity. There are many details to figure out over the coming weeks, and even months, as other teams and players determine their plans for next season.

A few closing thoughts:

- *I urge every player and parent to ask themselves, "What do I want next year?" This is the conversation I initiated with my family and, three weeks ago, with the other coaches on our team.*
- *I would like to talk with everyone one-on-one about what might be best for you and your son. I will try to initiate these conversations over the next week or so, but please don't feel you have to wait for me to call — I'm happy to discuss anytime (although I will be taking some vacation at the end of next week).*
- *I will do everything I can to help you find a situation next season that is a good fit for your son and family.*

Again, thank you for a fantastic season and I look forward to our team party in July where we can celebrate the great improvements and successes of the team and the individual players.

Coach Dan

Making a Difference

I still feel bad for my outburst after the game the other night. Shouting back at Robert and Debbie isn't the lasting image I want for the kids and parents to remember. But I do believe I've tried to be honest, fair, and open with everyone in this process. I really do want what is best for each kid, but I'm the first to accept that not everyone can have what they want all the time.

Although I look back on the explosion with Robert as the big disappointment of the season, I feel that I tried. Certainly I would do many things differently knowing what I do now. I'd still like to believe Robert and I can work it out, but now I need to move on.

The bottom line is that I feel good. The parents have been very supportive in the last 48 hours. In addition to the group that took me out for dinner and a beer, I received six emails. They've helped put the season in proper perspective.

Dan,
A few season ending thoughts....

Nicely handled on the announcement. Unfortunately, it was pretty obvious not everyone agreed. In my opinion, we're better off knowing now, and allowing us to begin finding a new team. As

I said the other night, I don't think (my son) is a majors level player, but if you run short of players and think he could help your squad, we'd love to play for you again — so don't rule us out!

Second, a heartfelt thank you for all of your efforts this year. At least in my opinion, you maximized the success the team could have, given our talent level. The kids had fun. And most importantly to me, MY kid had fun.

Third, a bit of unsolicited opinion (not advice). Some of the reaction from the parents absolutely amazes me. I think it is particularly ironic that a coach (maybe it was just his wife) who has been acting in the best of interest of their individual kid all year would find fault in your announcement and correct assessment of the situation. Alan is ready to move up. It's not just the stats. Again opinion, but Alan is the most improved player on the team. He was absolutely solid to start with, and just got better. Not a little bit, his improvement was constant, and significant.

It's been a pleasure, Dan — Good luck to you and your family, and thanks again for everything this year.

* * *

Dan,
As I have said before, although your explanation is appreciated, it is not necessary. We enjoyed the season and made some new friends; can't ask for much more!! (Our son) will play fall ball and then we will look into some off-season programs to prepare for next year. Again, we thank you and your staff for your commitment to the boys and we look forward to hearing your thoughts about next season.

* * *

Dan,

There is no easy way to address the subject matter that involves "this is over and we are moving on." Alan certainly deserves a shot at the majors. He is a wonderful boy and a great player. The "curse" of being a volunteer youth sports coach is that you are never going to make all of the parents happy, ever. Regardless of the enormous amount of time one spends coaching and organizing behind the scenes, a volunteer youth parent coach almost never "wins" in the end. Across all sports, it's a thankless job and unless you win 90% of the games and championships, it appears to be an unsuccessful year for some odd reason? Do you really think all of these parents are trying to live vicariously through their kids? Do they really think U12 baseball gets you a college scholarship or something? The work is just beginning at U12!

(Husband) and I spoke last night and consider this to be a tremendously successful year for our family. (Our son) loved baseball. He is sad it's over and wants to play more. He improved, he learned, he made new friends who he is eager to go to school with this fall. He stretched himself farther than he thought possible mentally from beginning to end. He was looking at his first stats report last night and said "I was awful." I batted "0" in 7 out of the first 8 games (something like that).

By the end he rarely struck out, had a considerable number of hits and we are calling it his "curse" that the balls kept getting fielded. With practice, those balls will stop getting fielded, and the curse will be broken. He feels he has the potential to be a great baseball player. When all is said and done, his confidence to swing the bat and hit the ball is firmly in place. His desire to get better is admirable. Sometimes as a youth sports coach you have to count the little victories, and he can be one of yours this year. Thanks for a great year coach Dan, and thanks for providing him this opportunity.

* * *

Hey Dan,
I thought I'd let the dust settle just a tad before I talked to you. Last night didn't seem quite appropriate. I want to thank you for the time and effort you've invested. Under the best of circumstances, I know it can be incredibly trying. Throw in some adversity and it can get downright crazy. You handled yourself, and the team, well throughout.

I appreciate you giving (our kid) a shot at this team . . . he had a great time this year, and I think it's really helped him focus on what he wants out of baseball in the future . . . as for your decision for next year, and your decision to announce it to the team last night, I can only wish you and Alan nothing but the best. I certainly don't blame you for doing what you believe is best for Alan's future. Thanks again.

* * *

Dan —
On behalf of our family, I want to thank you for a wonderful season. (Our son) really had fun and feels like he learned a lot. You're a wonderful coach and we appreciate what you have taught him this season . . . you kept it positive even when things weren't so positive and did a great job trying to keep parents and kids happy — not an easy job. We also appreciate your honesty regarding your goals for next season. We discussed it last night and (our son) would love to play for you again next season. We also understand if you feel he is not ready to play at the majors level, we'll defer to you on that.

Hey, Dan!
I just wanted you to know that I personally think you handled the situation beautifully. We were discussing it and there is no "perfect" way to say what you had to say, but I don't understand how or why anyone would be upset. Change happens and in the blink of an eye these boys will be in high school competing for 15 spots. The environment needs to be as challenging as possible to prepare them for this. Thanks for a great year. (Our son) is a better baseball player today than he was a year ago. He said last night that it was the most fun he's had playing yet, so know in his case you have done your job! Thanks again!

* * *

Had Abraham Lincoln been a baseball coach, he would have changed a few words in one of his most famous sayings. Saddled with the responsibilities of managing a team of 11 youth players, he might have declared:

You can please some of the parents all of the time, you can please all of the parents some of the time, but you can't please all of the parents all of the time.

I actually thought I had pulled off the latter. Yeah, there were a few ruffled feathers here or there, but the disagreements have been minimal. I'd like to attribute that to superb coaching and magnificent diplomacy . . . but, honestly, the success is actually more reflective of how we set the team up from the very beginning: **fun, learn, compete**.

I'm choosing to not let the conflict with Robert sour the kids' great season.

Part VI

July

July 8

World Series Umpires

Last night I went to the league's World Series championship and sat in the stands as a spectator. It was a great game; zero-zero going into the sixth inning. The final score was 3 - 2 and the catcher tagged out the tying run on a steal of home with the bases loaded to end the game. Plenty of drama and tension in that one inning!

The umpires for this game were excellent. The two kids (they were probably in their early 20s) acted professionally, effectively managed the pace of the game, were clear with their calls and signals, and communicated their expectations for players and coaches. Serious, yet willing to smile and joke with the coaches, each carried an authoritative presence that was equal to the importance placed on the game by the league and participants. Clearly, they were in control of the game.

As much grief as umpires take — some of it justified — it's important to remember that they are vital to the game of baseball. About 90 percent of the plays in any game are obvious and don't need an objective party to make a call. However, in the other 10 percent, umpires prevent constant argument and the outbreak of anarchy. Even when every call in a game is clear and easy, the mere presence of an umpire brings credibility to the contest.

We don't usually have umpires at informal scrimmages, but without the "blue" managing play and casting judgment, it is a completely different atmosphere. Even if, just like in regular games, players wear uniforms, we keep score, and reinforce how seriously kids should take the contest, play without an umpire lacks a certain credibility that only an impartial person can bring. Ultimately, I want an umpire to control the game so that the skill of the players and their on-the-field-performance determines the outcome. If coaches, fans, or umpires have too much influence it's the kids — and the game itself — that are cheated.

So what makes a good umpire? I umpired slow-pitch softball for 10 summers and I will be the first to say that it is not an easy job. I had to be focused and engaged on every pitch — if I zoned out for even one moment I could miss a call. This would immediately erode my credibility and move the focus from the players to me. I had to know all of the rules inside and out so that I could unwind a complicated play and make sure the rules were applied correctly. I also had to know where I needed to be on the field in any given situation to have the best vantage point to make the call. This meant starting each play in the right location and then moving quickly to get the proper angle to see the action. If I didn't, I could, at best, rightfully be criticized for not hustling and, at worst, miss a call because I couldn't see it.

It struck me, well after my rookie season, that umpires cannot watch the game like a fan. Fans are enjoying the beauty of the game, thinking about possibilities and outcomes. Players and coaches dig several layers deeper, quickly calculating tactical decisions and pondering strategy all the while taking note of fundamentals and mechanics for future instruction.

An umpire's experience of the game, though, is fundamentally different. There's an overall law-and-order environment he wants to create and maintain. The umpire does this by convincing players, coaches, and fans that he's getting the calls right. To do that, the umpire can't watch like a fan, player or coach. Umpires, rather, dissect a play in a unique way to determine where their next call (or calls) will be and bust tail to be in position to make it. If they are doing their job well, they are looking at snippets of the action, always a step ahead of where the ball might be to get in proper position to make next call.

As a result, umpires rarely get to watch the footwork of a shortstop snagging a ground ball in the hole. Rather, blue sees that the catch is made and then moves his body and fixes his gaze at first base to be stationary and focused to see who arrives first: ball or base runner's foot. If he watches the flight of the ball across the diamond (like fan, player and coach), his eyes and head will be moving when ball and runner arrive at the bag, making a good call very difficult. This means the umpire doesn't get to appreciate the effort of the batter hustling down the line or the strength of the shortstop's throw. The umpire's world is much more black and white: Where is the play going to be? Where should I be positioned to make the call? What rules apply? Safe or out? Fundamentals, outcomes, and meaning are for others to contemplate.

Again, it's not an easy job to get body, eyes, and mind all focused to make judgment on action that happens in less than the blink of an eye. I'm amazed when watching a game on TV how accurate major league umpires are with their calls. Slow motion replays show them getting the call right almost all of the time, even when my naked eyes initially said otherwise.

Unlike most other professions, success for an umpire doesn't just mean getting all the calls right. While that type of perfection is what they strive for, getting it wrong or right often depends solely on what dugout you sit in. The call of "safe" on a bang-bang play gets agreement from one team but groans (at best) from the other. So knowing in your heart you got it right might feel good as an umpire, but about half of the players, fans, and coaches believe you got it wrong. The righteousness of a call is just like beauty . . . it's in the eye of the beholder. Success then, has to be something more than getting them right.

In my days as a softball umpire, I learned to "see them as I call them." When Rich, the veteran umpire who trained me, said that phrase I was quick to point out that he had it backwards. Obviously, I thought, an umpire sees them and then calls them.

But this wise old sage looked at me patiently and said, "Dan, you're not going to get every call right. Nobody ever does. Not over the course of a long season. You have to convince everyone you know what you are doing. Hustle, get in position, focus on the play, and then make your call."

I can do that, I thought, already beginning to discredit his advice. That's what I saw other umpires do all the time. So what's the rub?

Sensing my skepticism, Rich continued, "But there are going to be times where you're not sure. Even though you were watching, you didn't really see it. The eyes saw action, but the brain didn't compute a call based on the data. Nothing will come to mind. For one reason or another, in that split second you have to decide, neither call will seem right."

He let that possibility hang in the air a moment and then finished me off. "Or worse, you'll see safe and yell out."

My world was rocked. Umpires weren't supposed to be constrained by the laws of us mere mortals. Darn it, they were supposed to have x-ray vision into plays and immediately shout out the right answers. Somehow I thought that the uniform, hat, or maybe the ball and strike indicator brought immunity to indecision.

At that moment I wasn't able to reconcile how umpires sometimes had made wrong calls in games I'd played or watched. But before I could ponder this gaping hole in my belief system, Rich laid more wisdom on me.

"If it is a close play that could go either way and you call it safe, see it that way and sell the call," he said. "Yes, you have to sell the call. Don't just say 'safe,' say 'safe — his foot was off the bag' if that's what you think happened. Make your calls more convincing. People might not like it, but they are more comfortable knowing you think you got it right and that you have rationale to back it up. Sell them on the idea that the right answer is clear in your mind. That's one of the ways you remain in charge of the game and keep the focus on the play on the field — not you. Because as soon as you show that you're unsure of a call, they'll eat you alive."

After 10 years of wearing the blue, I think he's right. See them as you call them.

Now this isn't an invitation for lazy umpires to just say whatever comes to mind and then, like a seventh grader without his homework, make up some lame rationale for the obvious mistake. Yes, that happens. It probably happens more times than it should (coaches fudge sometimes too, don't we?). But most umpires are good people doing their best at a difficult job. They get a large majority of the calls right. They deserve a little latitude . . . but only a little . . . after all, I'm now a coach!

All I ask from umpires is to hustle, know the rules, communicate clearly, and maintain a focus on doing what's right for the kids. Nail those and, at least in my book, the umpire earns the right to see them as he calls them.

So this begs the question . . . What's the best way for a coach to work with an umpire? Based on my experience of wearing the blue for 10 years and dealing with umpires this season, this is my advice:

1. ***Respect the role.*** Show respect for the role of umpire and the value they bring to the game. It is tough to have a fair game and feel good about the outcome unless you have an objective third party watch the action and make a ruling. Having a dad of the opposing team call your fastest kid out at the plate doesn't sit well when it was obvious he beat the throw and tag. Be glad you have an umpire keeping it fair.
2. ***Respect the person.*** The person wearing the uniform is a human being just like the rest of us (although I will admit that there may be times you want to question this . . . don't go there!). Accept in advance that this human is going to make mistakes.
3. ***Respect the game.*** Umpires love the game too. Respect it and they'll respect you.
4. ***Focus on the kids.*** You're in trouble if the umpire sees that your ego is larger and more important than the success and happiness of your players. Umpires see your motives better than players and parents. Take the approach that all of the adults on the field (coaches and umpires) are there to promote the enjoyment and development of the kids . . . you each have a role to play, but in an important way, you're all on the same team just doing different jobs.

5. ***Be reasonable.*** Don't argue every call (you know who you are!). Don't expect perfection. Don't expect to always get your way. Do try to problem-solve when conflict arises. When in doubt, let the umpire do his job — try not to do it for him.
6. ***Be polite.*** Ask for timeout and calmly walk out of the dugout to discuss an issue or raise a question. Don't come running out onto the field with guns blazing, no matter how right you think you are. An umpire wants — and needs — law and order, not the Wild, Wild West. You should want that too.
7. ***Laugh.*** Be willing to laugh at the crazy things that happen on the field. Be willing to laugh at yourself. Umpires are there to do a job, but they want to enjoy it, too. Having fun is what the game is about. Having a sense of humor shows the umpire that your priorities are straight.
8. ***Downsize your ego.*** You'll never win points by showing or telling the umpire you know more than he does (even when you do).
9. ***Focus on instructing the kids.*** No matter how badly the umpire blows a call that goes against you, there's a learning opportunity for your team. Run all the way through the bag . . . charge the ground ball . . . don't watch so many good pitches go by . . . throw more strikes . . . Role model to your kids to focus on the things you can change (effort and technique) not the things you can't (the call).

If coaches make these things part of their approach, they'll have few serious problems with umpires. Blue will still blow calls and cause occasional indigestion, but in the long run coaches and their teams will have a lot more fun.

Again, even though they wear blue and a short-brimmed hat, remember we're all on the same team . . . we're all trying to create the best possible youth baseball experience for the kids. It takes all of us working together.

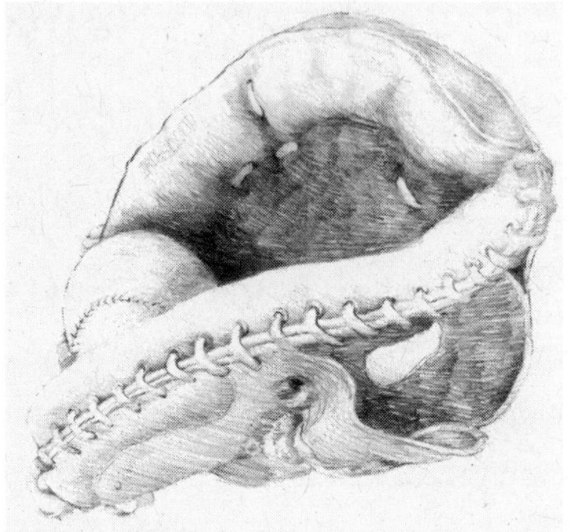

July 9

A Sad Ending to a Friendship — What I Learned

Robert's not a bad guy. I really believe that. If I felt that he was a jerk, then what does that say about the previous six years when I considered him a good friend? We coached together, we hung out together, and we even vacationed together. Those were good times. He may never speak to me again, but I'm not willing to toss those memories away or devalue them by simply writing him off as a rotten apple.

Nor do I think he transformed into a villain. He wasn't a rogue in hiding, just waiting for the opportune moment to shuck the camouflage and reveal his true character. People do change though. Their interests diverge or their life situation is somehow altered so that different things become important. This can happen abruptly. But I don't think that explains Robert's behavior either.

So what happened?

He made a string of poor choices, said several ugly things, and exhibited bad behavior. I'll probably never know what was going through his heart and mind in those two or three weeks. I have, though, been giving thought to how our friendship disintegrated so fast.

One possibility is that he wanted to coach and felt that my decision stole that from him. He may have believed it would be difficult to keep the rest of the team together or attract enough other players to compete at AAA. Another possibility is that he's had a few tough coaching situations over the years, dealing with parents and other coaches, and this may have opened old wounds. We've also had a super supportive group of parents and he may not have wanted to break them up. And I'm sure he wanted to have a good spot for his son. My guess is that he believed keeping the existing team together was the easiest option to get what he felt he needed.

Put all of these factors together and Robert likely felt heavily invested in the status quo. I am willing to bet that whatever he was feeling was similar to what a mother grizzly bear experiences when her cub is threatened. It's fast, aggressive behavior to protect her young.

My gut says Robert was encountering a lot of conflicting thoughts and emotions. Amid this complexity he was simply trying to protect the situation he believed would be best for Kaleb next season. I understand that. I respect that. However, I disagree with the method he and Debbie chose to do it. I feel a little like the innocent hiker who stumbles into a clearing to find momma grizzly on his right and baby bear on his left. Wrong place; wrong time.

My experience is that this momma grizzly phenomenon is universal among parents. Most will never have reason to show it. However, the behavior quickly surfaces the moment a situation doesn't feel like it is in the best interest of your kid. Bev and I both felt those raw emotions several years ago when Alan played football. He received almost no instruction but the coach frequently hollered at him for not doing things right. As an eight-year-old he didn't understand the game, had never been taught fundamentals, yet got an earful of yelling at practice. I remember feeling rage towards the coach and that we were being cheated by the experience. Fortunately Bev and I were able to rein in those emotions. We explained our feelings to the coach and it got a little better. Ultimately, we had to live with the situation until the end of the season.

These protective parental feelings of anger and frustration and a deep desire to shelter our child are simply part of being a human parent. We shouldn't try to repress them, nor should we act rashly on them. We need to recognize that they play an important motivational role — we might not be as critical of the situation or feel compelled to act if they weren't so powerful. So while they may feel "bad," they are actually giving us information and inspiration to change the situation. Then it comes down to *Respond* and *React.* Yes, the kid is the most important thing, but can I protect him in a way that also preserves the relationship and my integrity?

The situation with Robert has helped me realize that as coaches — volunteer coaches — we put ourselves at risk everyday. We're hiking in the woods, with what we hope is a loyal tribe following close behind. Our intentions are pure; we're excited about both the journey and destination. However, we must also be aware that at any given moment any of those families can turn "momma grizzly" on us. It can happen in an instant and we may never see it coming. There simply are so many other things going on around us in the forest, we're not always in tune with what's a threat and what's a harmless woodland creature. We're busy with schedules, uniforms, lineups, practice plans, equipment, logistics and the countless other things we can't let drop . . . and then, boom, there's momma grizzly . . .

I've learned that we are better at spotting hazards in the forest when we communicate and understand what's important to families and what's in their hearts and minds. We have to rely on parents to tell us what they're thinking and feeling. They have to alert us to danger. But they'll only do that if we have a solid relationship, they trust us and, often, only if we ask the right questions. I now appreciate that this primal power transforming an otherwise rational, thoughtful person into a momma grizzly is much stronger than the bonds of friendship.

My mistake was not enough meaningful communication with Robert. We talked a lot about the team, practice plans, and game strategy. I should have engaged him more about how things were going with Kaleb. I should have seen Robert's initial reluctance to discuss the issue as a red flag and changed the course of the conversation. I should have understood what the group of parents and the opportunity to coach this team meant to Robert. I should have been more aware of how on edge Robert and Debbie seemed to be. In that sense I may have failed them as coach.

July 28

Reflecting on a Perfect Season

I've had a couple of weeks to get away from baseball and the end of the season silliness. The break has been healthy. It has allowed me to regain my perspective on what we accomplished.

We had our end-of-the-season party, which was a bit weird. The undercurrent of Robert and Debbie's explosion cast a shadow over the event. I think everyone had fun at the event but the energy and enthusiasm that defined this group of parents and kids was gone. Although we were there to celebrate our accomplishments, we all realized that the nine-month ride was over. Nobody said those words, but the sentiment showed in everyone's demeanor. Conversations were quieter; smiles were fewer.

Even though the group was more subdued, we shared a definite feeling of satisfaction and contentment. It was the realization that we — parents, kids, and coaches — had a great, if not perfect, season. We took silent pride in the achievement of **fun, learn, compete** . . . collectively we were successful in creating an enjoyable and memorable baseball experience for our kids.

As I called up each kid to congratulate him on his season, I explained how I had seen them grow over the season, asked them to describe their favorite moment, and then I recounted something memorable they had done — a big hit, a great defensive play, a superb pitching performance.

As coach, it is these things, like the ones from my own youth, that I'll remember. The smiles, laughs, pressure packed wins, and tough losses. It's the characters, dramas, triumphs, defeats and funny things that were said and done. Yes, in my old age I'll remember Brandon's infectious smile after hitting one of his many triples and his infatuation with white Trident gum (which he thought was the secret to his success). I'll also recall that he got braces and couldn't chew gum . . . and for a while he felt like the Biblical hero Samson who lost his strength after getting his hair cut. Brandon though, was able to improvise with white Tic-Tacs and continue his torrid hitting streak.

I'll always smile when I see a relief pitcher give up a homerun . . . I'll be remembering Nick's grand slam early in our season. The other team brought in a new pitcher with the bases loaded. Nick crushed this poor kid's first pitch well over the 275-foot sign on the left field fence. I felt sad for the young pitcher as he hung his head in despair, and pure joy for Nick as he sped around the bases. It was a perfect example of the joy of victory and the agony of defeat.

The memories of Jaime's hit streak, Tylerville, Dillon's passion for the game, Zach earning a start on the mound, and Bobby's unbelievable pitching performance to start the season . . . these are just a few of the things I'll carry with me for the rest of my life. In addition to the fond memories, I've also grown and learned a tremendous amount this season that will make me a better coach. The biggest ongoing challenge was to *Respond* more and *React* less. I had success . . . I also had setbacks. Simple . . . not easy.

As I think about what instruction I would give on how to *Respond* more and *React* less, I have developed a checklist of four behaviors. Each has a simple question that helps me put the situation and my choices of words and actions in better perspective.

1. ***Creator*** — What kind of world do I want?
2. ***Seeker*** — What do I need to know?
3. ***Sender*** — What will happen?
4. ***Finisher*** — What am I prepared to do?

Creator

I realize that the single most important thing I did as coach this season was establish a clear vision for what we would accomplish as a team. Our shared definition of success — **fun, learn,** and **compete** — was the guiding light through the season, grounding me when decisions were difficult or emotions were running high. It also helped everyone else understand my actions and align their own behavior with our common purpose. As a coach of a team, I'm creating something new. A new season, a new experience, a new opportunity . . . what kind of world do I want? I'll need to answer that again this fall when I start putting together my new team.

Seeker

I can't know everything. Period. A good coach, or a person who *Responds* wisely, is a seeker of knowledge. A coach always needs to be investigating why . . . why is Jimmie struggling at the plate, why can't Johnny catch the fly balls, why do we seem to fall apart in the fourth or fifth inning, why can't Billy throw strikes.

In any situation, I can observe only so much. An enormous amount of information escapes my five senses, especially when things happen fast, are unexpected, or a strong emotion or bad assumption clouds my perception. At different times I assumed the kids knew how to slide, I assumed I'd never get tossed from a game (I'm not T*HAT* type of coach . . .), I assumed my friendship with Robert was rock solid. I was at my best — and our team had the most success — when I'd ask a question of the kids, coaches, or parents. The search for a more complete understanding of the situation made me a better communicator and well-rounded decision maker. The infusion of knowledge and perspective enabled me to see beyond my own narrow slices and focus on the larger team goals.

Sender

I see that coaches who *Respond* consider the consequences of their decisions before they act or open their mouths. As a coach, I lead the team. I set the tone and everyone looks to me for direction, so I need to constantly be thinking about the message and image I am sending, or communicating, to others. I didn't do a good job of this when I got ejected from the game . . . I sent the umpire, and eventually my entire team, the wrong message. I tried to do a better job of this when dealing with Robert . . . even though it ended badly with him, I don't have regrets about my behavior or feel guilty about my actions or intentions. I see that I can't always control the outcome, but I can control my message and the impression I project to others.

Finisher

Follow through is usually what differentiates success from failure. Almost by definition, *Responding* is more difficult than *Reacting* (I don't have to think, ask questions, consider consequences . . . just act!). I realized this season that there were many required tasks that were difficult, unpleasant, painful, thankless, or otherwise undesirable . . . It's easier to not have that conversation with the parent, so I'll let the behavior slide. I'm tired of telling him to charge the ball at shortstop, so I'll either let him fail or move someone else into that position. Changing his throwing motion from sidearm to over the top is becoming too difficult.

Often in the heat of the moment we're willing to settle for less than we originally wanted. We'll take 75 percent of the goal because achieving 100 percent (or even 90 percent) would be too tough. We'll sacrifice quality in favor of the simple, easy, or less painful. This is a *Reaction.* I realized though that these unpleasant things had to be done if I was going to accomplish my goals.

As the leader of the team, I have to model follow through. I must show tenacity, discipline and *arête* — the Greek word meaning a personal sense of excellence in what we do. If I'm not willing to do these things, then I need to change my goals and priorities and create a different world.

These four behaviors will become my mental checklist to *Respond* more wisely . . . ***Creator, Seeker, Sender, Finisher***. Again, simple . . . but not easy! And there are four warning signs that I'm stuck in *React* mode . . . ***Selfish, Emotional, Rutted,*** and ***Cranial Bypass.*** This will be my blueprint to guide my decisions, actions, and words next season.

As I thumb through my journal entries I see that I learned many other things:

1. ***Fun, Learn, Compete works.*** This was a great framework for our team. I'll use it again next season, although depending on the makeup of the team and what we want to achieve, I'll likely define the terms a little differently to reflect the age, competitive level, talent, and aspirations.
2. ***Get the team right.*** Making good decisions about parents and kids is critical. The goals of the parents need to align with mine. Pure talent is only one of many considerations and certainly not the most important . . . ensuring that kids are at the correct competitive level is essential.
3. ***Play multiple sports.*** The kids should play other sports for as long as they want to and as long as they can. Forcing them to specialize in one sport is a tragedy that most will regret years later.
4. ***Wood bats are best.*** Congress should outlaw metal and ensure that talent and effort result in success. Lawmakers should eliminate the pathetic hollow tinks and restore the wholesome crack of the bat to the youth game. I will rant to anyone willing to listen . . . anyone up for a Constitutional amendment? How about a million bats march on Washington . . . who's with me?
5. ***Coaches must lead.*** The role of the coach is to lead the team. I must drive my vision — if I don't, the kids drift towards entropy and chaos or execute someone else's vision.
6. ***Set clear expectations and follow through.*** If I don't like performance or behavior, I must correct it and reset the expectations — for individuals and the team. It doesn't happen on its own.

7. ***Teach my son to slide.*** Once we get snow on the ground, Alan will spend the winter practicing his sliding. He will likely be doing pushups instead of making snow angels . . .
8. ***Yelling does not help.*** A player knows when he makes a mistake. My job is to help him understand what fundamentals need to be improved to shore up the performance. The statistical concept of regression towards the mean will bring their next effort closer to their average level of performance. Yelling only dampens the kids' spirit. Encouragement and instruction equate to high enthusiasm and long-term improvement.
9. ***Speak softly and tread lightly with umpires.*** Because my competitive juices flow easily, I must constantly be mindful to act like the role model I aspire to be . . . and aware that Bev will be there to not-so-gently correct my behavior.
10. ***Instruction should be specific.*** Generalities like, "You have to make a good throw," are the hallmark of Captain Obvious. I need to help them understand the what, how, and why.
11. ***The kids will underperform at times.*** I can't take it personally and must realize that the coach can't want it more than the players, nor can I do it for them. If I've fueled their passions, set expectations, instructed the proper techniques, and put them in positions in which they can succeed, then I've done my job . . . then they have to do theirs. Usually they will; sometimes they won't. When that happens, don't blow a gasket — keep the enthusiasm high.
12. ***Be humble.*** If you think the game of baseball is easy, go take batting practice or field 25 ground balls. The next day, the ibuprofen will only help the aching muscles, not the bruised ego. I must empathize with the kids when they fail and I must reinforce the need to keep trying.

It may be a simple game . . . but it's not easy. And remember, the ball *WILL* find the weak, injured, or unprepared.

13. ***Baseball is a game of family and generations.*** My success and love for the game is thanks to the coaches who spent their time on me . . . my efforts as coach pay it forward. I'm building memories to last a lifetime and developing the next generation of coaches.
14. ***Some coaches and parents simply want conflict.*** They thrive on argument and disagreement . . . I must always *Respond* wisely and engage only when absolutely necessary.
15. ***Fruits of your labors.*** I might work my tail off with a player, but it might not click for another year or two. The next coach will enjoy the fruit of my labor . . . and that's okay, it works that way sometimes. I did my job, and ultimately we're all on the same team, trying to get the kid where he needs to be.
16. ***Avoid confusion.*** Be clear with parents about giving instruction. I need to make sure parents inform me when they are telling their kid to do something. Preferably, they will leave instruction to the coaches and simply cheer enthusiastically for the team. That way the player isn't confused or caught in the middle.
17. ***Don't live vicariously.*** It's about the kids. I shouldn't place unhealthy expectations on Alan based on what I was — or was not — able to accomplish myself. It's about giving him the opportunity to accomplish what he wants to.
18. ***Kids should have fun.*** I realize more than ever that we are here simply to give each kid the best baseball experience possible . . . the level isn't important. As adults our victory is that they get to have success playing the game they love. That's what they'll remember 25 years from now — not that they won 14 games at the AAA level.

Put them at the highest level at which they can have success and savor the moments.

19. ***Learn life lessons.*** I see my job as one to help kids transfer knowledge gained on the field to all other aspects of their lives. The perfect example is Zach learning the connections between hard work, discipline, and the need to deal with failure. Earning the start as pitcher will be something he remembers for the rest of his life and hopefully, trigger successful behavior on and off the field.
20. ***Right vs. Effective.*** It is more important to be effective in accomplishing goals than to be right. After I got tossed, I could have argued with the umpire (again), about being right. An apology was effective in being a good role model and not getting reported to the league.
21. ***Umpires are people too.*** I need to remember to treat them with respect and show that I'm in it for the kids. They have a very difficult job and one that adds tremendous value to the game.
22. ***Communicate.*** My biggest responsibility is to communicate with players, parents, coaches, and umpires. Communicate, communicate, communicate! As a leader, I can't do too much of it.
23. ***Focus on the journey, not the end.*** We're there to help the kids have fun, learn the game, and experience the thrill of competition. It's that day-to-day, moment-to-moment journey that is important . . . not the final win-loss record.
24. ***It takes a community.*** I realize now that we're all on the same team. Parents, kids, coaches, umpires, and league officials have different roles and are on rival teams, but in a larger sense we're all working to give all of our kids a great baseball experience. We are all connected. Turning a blind eye to a dangerous situation or remaining silent when something is wrong harms us all.

25. ***Be careful of the momma grizzly.*** No relationship is safe in a youth sports environment. Every parent is in it first for his/her kid — don't forget that.

In the end, I'm just like the other 10 parents on the team — I too, am in it for my kid. I just get to be closer to it than most. I'm there for every practice and every game and consider myself fortunate to see it all … the good, the bad, and the ugly. It is a privilege to teach Alan the game I love and try to infuse my sense of how it should be played and respected. I have the great fortune to be there when the light bulb goes on . . . my journal entry from April 18 sums it up:

Alan's Homerun

Alan hit his first-ever out-of-the-park homerun last night in the game against the Sharks. In the first inning he came up with one on and one out. He took a ball and then fouled off three straight pitches. Alan hit the next one over the right-centerfield fence, clearing the chain-link by a good 10 feet. He wore a huge grin as he ran towards me at third base and gave me a high-five as he rounded the bag and headed home to greet his teammates. He was the center of the mob all the way back to the dugout. Alan deserves it; he's put in the effort and now has the results. It is a great life lesson.

Alan's joyful gaze told a story of a kid who worked exceptionally hard at being a better hitter. His sense of accomplishment stood on top of all those hours in the batting cage perfecting his swing. For perhaps the first time in his life he was enjoying the dividends of determination, hard work, and sweat.

Although I'll carry a strong memory of his trot and smile, I will forever cherish the sense of pride in his eyes that simply said, "I did it!" As third base coach, I was the only human being to see it. Alan ran straight towards me between second and third base and I was close enough to see the twinkle in his eyes. It was a small window . . . had I been in the stands I would have only seen the smile. And by the time he reached home plate this raw, fleeting, virgin emotion was overcome by celebration with friends.

Coaching a youth baseball team often means a long stream of thankless work, but being there for a moment like that with your son makes every bit of it worthwhile.

One parent's wisdom to me after the game is sage advice for us all: "Cherish these moments, Dan. Enjoy it for what it is. You never know how many you'll get . . . savor every one of them."

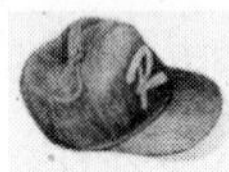

Epilogue

The Following July

It's hard to believe it has been a year since the mighty Yellow Jackets played their last game. In those 12 months, I formed a new team and we had another "perfect season," again, perfect in giving the kids what they needed, not so much in the win-loss record (although that was greatly improved this time around).

Of the 11 kids that played for me last season, six stayed together and moved up to the majors level. I merged with another AAA team, taking on five of their players and the head coach as one of my assistants. It looked to be a good fit: they lacked pitching and had several holes in their batting lineup; we were strong in pitching but couldn't play defense. Our theory was to combine our strengths for a formidable batting lineup, depth in pitching, and a solid defense.

It actually played out something close to that (although we still were a weak defensive squad). We played 48 games (about eight too many), finishing with a 31 - 17 record. We won a weekend tournament, besting 17 other teams for the big trophy and finished second in two others. We finished third in our league and made the playoffs. We lost in the first round and I was dangerously close to getting tossed for arguing a call that squelched our last-gasp rally. Looking back on it, I probably deserved to get the heave-ho. In my defense, however, the umpire agreed that our player's line drive did, in fact, hit the white line. He still ruled, though, that it was a foul ball . . . *apoplectic.*

Although hoisting the trophy after winning the tournament championship was a thrill, the highlight of the season for me as a coach and parent was about 12 games into the season. Up to that point Alan had continued his slide-avoidance behavior and, after losing it with him one evening, I made him side continually in the grass in our neighbor's yard the next day. (Sliding on our xeriscaped yard might have added to his slide-avoidance behavior ...) In the game that night he was on third base and I told him he had to try to score if the pitch got away from the catcher.

Sure enough, the next pitch squirted under the catcher's glove all the way to the backstop. Alan lumbered toward the plate, and, as if he'd been doing it his whole life, slid in safe under the tag. He received a raucous standing ovation from our stands. Our parents showered him with whistles, shouts, and applause, all of which were way over the top for scoring a run, yet fitting for finally completing a multi-year project. As he jogged back to the dugout he had a bewildered look on his face — a mixture of surprise at the act being so easy, pride that he'd finally done it, and embarrassment that it had taken him so long to do it. His score gave us a six-run lead and I felt compelled to explain to the other coach that we weren't cheering for a blowout. Once he knew the back-story, he smiled and, despite being behind by a touchdown, seemed pleased he'd been a witness to such a momentous accomplishment.

On a less enjoyable note, my relationship with Robert apparently is going to end up like Humpty Dumpty — I'm no longer hopeful that we'll be able to put it back together again. He still has no interest whatsoever in talking to me and he refuses to acknowledge my "hi's" or waves when I see him around town. While I'm sad and disappointed over the loss of a good friendship, I sleep well knowing I've done what I can. I'll remain open to reconciling our differences, but I'm not going to spend any more of my life's energy worrying about it. Life is too short; there are many more productive ways to spend my time.

I talked to a coaching buddy, Jake, about a similar decision he faced with his team at the end of last season. He had a few kids who wanted more of a competitive challenge and to play more games. However seven of the kids/families desired something less. Since many of the kids had been together for several years, Jake spent a lot of time to find another coach that was forming a team that would be a good fit for the other seven. When Jake told the team of his decision, he had four happy sets of parents . . . and seven who were irate. Despite his efforts to get them what they wanted, he was still "the bad guy" for leaving them. He told me recently that only one parent in the seven families will speak to him, and it's now a year later. Jake stumbled into a whole den of momma grizzlies.

This points to an ongoing issue in youth sports — how to effectively deal with transitions. Changes will be necessary, for all of the reasons I outlined before about abilities and interests. No matter how good the intentions, coaches are in a delicate spot. My approach didn't work well for at least one family on my team. Jake's attempt alienated seven — and he put more effort into it than I did. Communication is critical, but it won't solve all situations. That's the territory coaches inhabit. Ultimately we must realize that not all leaders are beloved by all . . . do your best and move on. Again, life is too short to worry about the insecurities, expectations, and behavior of others.

I also learned that even a year isn't long enough to wipe the slate completely clean. Towards the end of our season Bev was trying to explain to my daughter Rachel where Alan's game was to be played that night. Innocently enough, Bev said, "It's over at the field where Alan hit his homerun out of the park."

That didn't ring a bell for Rachel. She contorted her face as she thought about it for a while, and then, in a great ah-ha moment smiled and said, "Oh, is that the park where Daddy got tossed?" Coaching reputations, it seems, don't die . . . or fade away . . .

Like last year at this time, I'm exhausted, ready for a mental and physical break . . . and at the same time anxious for the new season to start. It will likely be my last as a youth coach, at least of Alan. After a shortened spring season, I'll wipe a tear from my eye as I hand the kids off to the high school coaches for summer ball. But the four months I'll get with the kids will be the next chapter in my love affair with the game of baseball. It's another season on the diamond — I give thanks for this gift and blessing . . . play ball!

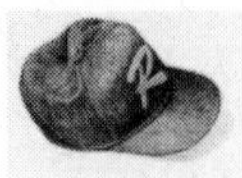

Acknowledgements

First, a heartfelt thanks to all of the players and families who were a part of this Perfect Season. As I said at the end of the ride, coaching these boys was one of the most rewarding experiences of my life . . . thank you for the opportunity.

I also owe eternal gratitude to all of my coaches from tee ball through college . . . thanks for teaching me the game, encouraging me to work hard, and most importantly, fueling my passion for baseball.

Thanks also to the people who helped turn this manuscript into a book. Judith Briles and John Maling, your insights and editorial guidance were invaluable in helping me both stay sane and reach the destination. Nick Zelinger, I appreciated your enthusiasm and strong sense of design — both show in the final product.

I can't imagine undertaking a project like this without the support of my family. Mom, Dad, Laurie, Grandma, Dick, and Betty, thanks for believing in me and offering constant encouragement. And Mom, the baseball drawings you created for this book are outstanding — thank you. You are an immensely talented artist!

And finally, to my home team who had to live with me throughout this project . . .

Rachel, thanks for understanding how much time it is to coach. I know I've missed out on some of your activities with Cody (the horse), but believe me, they are just as important as Alan's baseball! You'll have to forgive me though . . . I'll have trouble writing a book like this about horseback riding.

Alan, thanks for the opportunity to be your coach. Thanks for trying hard, working hard, and sharing the great game with me. I treasure our seasons together. Also, thanks for your ongoing efforts to slide at bases . . .

Bev, thanks to my true partner. I could not have done this without you. You always seemed to know just when I needed your ideas and your instincts were always right on. Thanks for the encouragement and belief in the book . . . and my ability to complete it. Your support was more important than you'll ever know. Thank you.

About Coach Dan

Dan Clemens has coached youth baseball for nine years, starting with five-year-old tee-ballers up through 13-year-olds. He's also coached youth basketball, football and soccer.

Less concerned with wins and losses, Dan's philosophy is that all youth sports should embody three things:

1. Kids should **learn** about the game, teamwork, and themselves;
2. Kids should be **competitive** (play at the appropriate level as individuals and a team); and
3. Kids should, above all, have **fun**.

If youth coaches accomplish those three things, he says, we produce healthy, happy kids, ready to enter high school with experiences and fond memories to last a lifetime.

By day, Dan works with *Fortune* 500® companies, medium-sized businesses, and non-profit organizations to develop leaders and help them communicate more effectively both as individuals and organizations. A core theme in his work is helping leaders understand the key differences between *Responding* and *Reacting.* He believes a leader *Responds* wisely to the opportunities in a situation, rather than simply *Reacting* to his/her narrow experience of it. A member of the National Speakers Association, he also brings the message of **fun, learn, compete** and ***Respond*** vs. ***React*** to keynote presentations and workshops across the country.

About Coach Dan

Dan was an all-state baseball player his junior and senior years of high school and was on scholarship at a Division I University before a shoulder injury ended his baseball career. He's been a softball umpire for 10 years and a basketball referee for five years. He plays competitive baseball in an adult league, has run four marathons, and climbed 50 of the 54 mountain peaks in Colorado that rise above 14,000 feet. He lives in Colorado with his wife Bev and two kids, Alan and Rachel.

He maintains a Web site for coaches: www.coachclemens.com.